Social Media and Cultural Influence: Trends and Implications

Imran Khan

Copyright © [2023] by Imran Khan

Title: Social Media and Cultural Influence: Trends and Implications

Author: Imran Khan

All rights reserved. No part of this publication may be reproduced, distributed, or transmitted in any form or by any means, including photocopying, recording, or other electronic or mechanical methods, without the prior written permission of the publisher, except in the case of brief quotations embodied in critical reviews and certain other noncommercial uses permitted by copyright law.

This book is a work of fiction. Names, characters, places, and incidents are the product of the author's imagination or are used fictitiously. Any resemblance to actual events, locales, or persons, living or dead, is entirely coincidental.

ISBN: 978-93-5868-207-6

Cover design by Miss Anaya

Table of Content

Chapter 1: Introduction   05
- Introduction to the book's theme and purpose.
- Brief overview of the significance of social media in contemporary society.
- The impact of social media on culture and society.
- The structure of the book and what readers can expect from each chapter.

Chapter 2: The Evolution of Social Media   18
- A historical perspective on the development of social media platforms.
- Key milestones and innovations in the field.
- The role of technology in shaping social media.
- The growth and diversification of social media users.

Chapter 3: Social Media and Cultural Dynamics   34
- Exploration of how social media platforms affect cultural trends.
- Case studies on how social media has shaped cultural movements, including fashion, music, and language.
- The role of influencers and celebrities in cultural shifts.
- Discussion of the global nature of social media and its impact on cultural diversity.

Chapter 4: The Influence of Social Media on Identity and Self-Expression   51
- Examination of how social media platforms impact individual and group identities.
- Analysis of the impact on self-esteem and self-perception.
- The concept of "digital selves" and the implications for personal branding.
- Consideration of the positives and negatives of social media in terms of self-expression.

Chapter 5: The Implications for Society and Policy   67

- Discussion of the societal consequences of the widespread use of social media.
- Exploration of issues related to privacy, misinformation, and cyberbullying.
- Analysis of government and industry responses and regulations.
- A look at potential future policies and regulations to address social media's impact on society.

Chapter 6: The Future of Social Media and Cultural Influence   83
- Speculation on the future trends in social media.
- The role of emerging technologies (e.g., virtual reality, augmented reality) in shaping social media.
- Ethical considerations and potential positive and negative outcomes.
- Reflection on the book's main themes and a call to action for readers to engage critically with social media and its cultural implications.

Conclusion   99
- Summarization of the key points from each chapter.
- Final thoughts on the evolving relationship between social media and culture.
- The lasting impact of social media on society and the importance of responsible use.
- Encouragement for readers to continue exploring this dynamic field.

Chapter 1: Introduction

- **Introduction to the book's theme and purpose**

    Every book has its own individual message and goal in the broad world of literature. The theme and aim of a book serve as its basis, defining the narrative, characters, and ideas within its pages. Our investigation delves into the fascinating world of themes and goals, illuminating their significance in the realms of narrative and information transfer.

    Theme Statement
    The central idea or feeling that drives the story forward is known as the book's theme. It's the story's driving force, the thing everyone is talking about. Love, friendship, courage, redemption, societal conflicts, and existential musings are just a few examples of possible themes. The story's essence can be better grasped when the story's theme is clearly articulated and serves as a lens through which the story's events and characters can be interpreted.

    Discovering Meaning
    While a book's topics are its intellectual and emotional backbone, the book's purpose is what drives its creation. Authors embark on their creative travels with various purposes, be it to entertain, educate, provoke thinking, challenge society conventions, or push for change. When readers know why they're reading a book, they're better able to analyze it critically and get fully invested in the subject matter.

    The Reflective Power of Literature on Culture
    In many ways, literature is a reflection of the times in which it was produced. They are powerful means of commenting on society and illuminating the issues, ideas, and cultural nuances of the time. Authors illustrate the nuances of the human experience via skillfully

weaved ideas and deliberate storytelling, evoking empathy and compassion in their readers. Literature thus serves as a unifying force in the face of cultural and generational differences.

Purpose and Central Ideas across Genres
Thematic and functional questions can be probed in a variety of ways, depending on the genre. To keep readers on the edge of their seats, a mystery novel's central theme could center on the search for truth and justice. Science fiction explores ideas of the future and frequently considers the moral implications of new technologies. Romance books delve into the nuances of interpersonal relationships and center on universal themes like love, trust, and fortitude. Authors can appeal to a wider range of readers with different expectations and tastes by tailoring their work to various genres.

Empowering Readers and Igniting Change Books offer the potential to inspire change. Authors who skillfully weave stories around issues of social injustice, equality, or environmental conservation can spark debate, confront biases, and galvanize audiences to take action. Literature can serve as a catalyst for social advancement when its themes and goals are in harmony, prompting its readers to examine their own values and consider how they might make a good difference in the world.

The Road Ahead
We delve into the brains of authors and the complexities of their works as we set out on this journey into literary themes and intentions. We examine the impact of themes on character development, story progression, and reader engagement. We analyze the impact that books with varying goals—from diversion to education—have on the literary world.

In the next chapters, we'll examine concrete works of ancient and current literature to determine what it is that makes them so enduring. In doing so, we want to gain a deeper appreciation for the craft of storytelling and an awareness of literature's transformative power in both individual lives and collective communities.

The study of literature's themes and goals is, in sum, a fascinating activity because it provides windows into the human condition, the workings of society, and the potency of language. When readers have a firm grasp of these factors, they are able to connect with novels on a more profound level, better appreciating the author's meticulous consideration of every word. Let us, as we flip through books, appreciate the wide range of topics and goals explored by authors, and hail the power of literature to expand our horizons and deepen our understanding of the world.

- **Brief overview of the significance of social media in contemporary society**

  The rise of social media in the digital age has had a profound impact on people's methods of interaction with one another and their understanding of the world around them. Social media's meteoric development has altered the very nature of human communication, reshaping not just interpersonal interactions but also the professional, academic, political, and activist spheres. This essay delves deeply into the various ways in which the rise of social media has affected modern society as a whole, from the perspective of both individuals and local and global communities.

  I. Globalization and Social Networking
  Distances between people of different cultures and origins have been reduced because to the availability of real-time communication tools made possible by social media. It's changed what we think of as social networking by making it possible to keep in touch with people across great distances and in different time zones. Photos and videos allow distant family members to feel closer by sharing memories together. In addition, the global community is now more interconnected than ever before because to the spread of ideas and cultural practices through social media.

  Part Two: Interaction and Sharing of Information
  The speed with which information can be shared is one of the most significant effects of social media. News, events, and developments from around the world can be disseminated within seconds, allowing individuals to keep updated about current affairs. As a forum for public debate and discussion, users of social media sites can air their views on important cultural and political topics. A better educated and involved citizenry is a direct result of the democratization of knowledge.

Thirdly, Commerce and Marketing
In terms of advertising, promotion, and interaction with customers, social media has been a game-changer for businesses. Targeted advertisements allow businesses to reach a large audience, which in turn increases brand recognition and consumer loyalty. Twitter and Facebook allow for direct communication with customers, while platforms like Instagram and Pinterest have proven indispensable for visual marketing. The rise of social media influencers as influential marketing tools has influenced customer behavior. Small businesses may now compete with larger ones thanks to the low barrier to entry and high return on investment provided by social media marketing.

E-Learning and the Future of Education
The influence of social media on learning has been revolutionary. It has helped pave the way for online learning platforms, giving students access to books, videos, and courses regardless of their location. High-quality education is now available to a global audience because to the rise of Massive Open Online Courses (MOOCs). Students and teachers are better able to work together because to the increased communication made possible by social media. There is now no distinction between digital and traditional classrooms because to innovations like online discussion forums and virtual lecture halls.

The Mobilization of Society and Politics
Providing a forum for underrepresented groups and community organizations, social media has been instrumental in recent political and social revolutions. Social media has been instrumental in elevating awareness and participation in movements such as the Arab Spring, #BlackLivesMatter, and #MeToo. Activists can rally support, bring attention to pressing social problems, and take on entrenched authorities. Social media platforms serve as catalysts for

change, enabling individuals to organize protests, share petitions, and engage in lobbying initiatives. Election campaigns and lobbying efforts around the world have shown the impact that social media may have on public opinion and political outcomes.

Consequences for Emotional Health and Happiness
While there are many positive aspects of social media, there are also some worries about how it may affect users' psychological well-being. The continual exposure to controlled and idealized representations of others' lives can lead to feelings of inadequacy and low self-esteem, especially among younger users. Problems such as cyberbullying, social comparison, and FOMO (fear of missing out) are common in the online world. Furthermore, the constant scrolling and notifications that are hallmarks of social networking platforms can add to stress and reduce productivity. The detrimental impacts of social media on mental health can be reduced by addressing these concerns and fostering digital literacy and mindfulness.

Conclusion
In conclusion, social media has become deeply embedded in today's culture, profoundly influencing how we talk to one another and understand the world around us. Its importance may be seen in many spheres, from intimate interactions and formal learning to professional settings and social movements. Among the many benefits of social media to contemporary society are the democratization of information, the amplification of voices, and the interconnectedness of worldwide communities. However, it is necessary to acknowledge the issues it offers, particularly in terms of mental health and digital well-being.

Finding a middle ground between social media's advantages and disadvantages is crucial as society continues to negotiate the challenges of the digital age. Essential measures toward optimizing the good impact of social media include educating users about responsible online behavior, promoting digital literacy, and encouraging a healthy relationship with the platform. Modern society may continue to adapt and grow in the digital age if its members learn to use social media to its full potential while also overcoming its problems.

- **The impact of social media on culture and society**

    The fast development of social media platforms over the past few of decades has had a profound impact on societal organization, communication, and interaction. The way we think, feel, and act are all influenced by social media's pervasive presence in today's culture. This essay delves at the many ways in which social media has affected our society and culture, including its effects on our sense of self, how we interact with others, and the values we uphold as a society.

    I. Creating a New Digital Self
    The boundaries between the online and offline worlds have become increasingly porous as a result of the proliferation of social media. People craft their online identities, highlighting some characteristics while hiding others. The need to uphold a given image is exacerbated when biased reporting leads to the creation of glorified personas. As a result, social media has promoted a climate wherein individuals constantly evaluate themselves in relation to others. Additionally, the emergence of online communities and subcultures has allowed individuals to interact based on shared interests, hobbies, or identities, leading to the formation of new cultural affiliations and subcultural movements.

    Modifying Interactional Routines
    The widespread use of social media platforms has had a revolutionary effect on human interaction. Social networking sites like Facebook, Twitter, and Instagram make it simple to keep in constant contact with friends and family from anywhere in the world, regardless of time or distance. Therefore, it has become easier to have conversations and make connections with people all over the world. However, the shortness and informality of online communication has also contributed to the development of digital

slang and abbreviations, which have influenced shifts in established patterns of speech.

Reconfiguring Social Interactions

Online and offline friendships have been revolutionized by social media. People are increasingly forming ties and friendships with one another online, thanks to the ease with which they may find others who share their interests and experiences. Relationships of substance can develop between people of different locations thanks to these online interactions. Cyberbullying, online harassment, and the decline of personal privacy are only some of the difficulties brought about by the internet. Also, people may put more stock in their online identities than in their real-life connections as a result of the constant interconnection made possible by social media.

Changing Traditional Values and Contemporary Practices

The fashion, art, music, and pop culture industries are just some of the areas that have been profoundly impacted by the rise of social networking. Global audiences are quickly captivated by viral challenges, memes, and internet movements. Celebrities and people who have a large following on social media have a lot of sway over the direction of products and the expectations of the public. Moreover, social media sites provide a voice for underrepresented groups to challenge status quo and push for social change through artistic and political expression. Movements like #Oscarssowhite and LGBTQ+ advocacy campaigns demonstrate the efficacy of social media in amplifying marginalized voices and fostering popular acceptance.

Difficulties and Moral Issues

While social media delivers numerous benefits, it also presents various obstacles and ethical considerations. Polarization and societal uncertainty have emerged as serious consequences of the proliferation of misinformation and fake news. Questions regarding digital security and individual autonomy are raised by incidents of privacy violation, data mining, and online spying. In addition, the addictive features of social media, such as the continual notifications and feedback loops, can have a negative effect on users' mental health and wellbeing, especially among younger users. Education about digital literacy, government oversight, and responsible platform policies are all necessary to solve these problems.

Conclusion
Social media has had far-reaching effects on culture and society, altering how people see themselves, interact with one another, and develop new social norms. Understanding the pros and downsides of social media use is crucial for thriving in today's online world. An informed, inclusive, and ethically conscious digital society can emerge by embracing the promise for positive change while tackling the issues it offers.

Societies may use the power of social media to amplify different voices, challenge stereotypes, and establish meaningful connections by boosting digital literacy, encouraging critical thinking, and cultivating responsible online behavior. To foster a positive and inclusive online community in today's hyper-connected world, it's important to have a firm grasp of the nuanced effects that social media has on culture and society.

- **The structure of the book and what readers can expect from each chapter**

In this literary adventure, we delve deeply into a wide range of topics, from the nuances of interpersonal relationships to the complexity of societal dynamics to the beauties of the natural world. The book has been precisely organized, providing a carefully curated arrangement of chapters that go into diverse facets of the selected themes, to help readers navigate this rewarding experience. This article gives a detailed synopsis of the book, outlining what each section contains and why it's important.

A. Contextualization I. Introduction

The introductory chapter acts as the cornerstone of the book, presenting readers with a roadmap for the future exploration. In this section, the book's overall themes and goals are presented, providing a preview of the essential ideas that will be discussed in length. The introduction lays forth the book's theoretical frameworks, major questions, and historical background. The opening provides a thorough summary, setting the stage for an enjoyable and educational read.

Part Two, First Chapter: The Decay of Social Connections

Love, friendship, betrayal, and redemption are just few of the themes that get a thorough examination in this first chapter. This chapter delves into the subtleties of interpersonal connections, using narratives and character studies to provide light on the feelings, motivations, and conflicts that form human bonds. Here, authors from the past and present give unique insights on the universal themes of love and connection through in-depth analyses of canonical literary partnerships.

Norms, prejudices, power conflicts, and societal evolution are all topics explored in Chapter 2's foray into the domain of societal dynamics. This chapter explores the complexities of social institutions and their effects on individuals and societies through a close reading of seminal works of fiction and nonfiction. The complicated human experience in a variety of social circumstances will be explored via discussions of topics including inequality, prejudice, and social justice.

Nature and the Natural World, Chapter Four
The third chapter delves deep into nature's wonders, discussing topics like climate change, biodiversity, and humankind's impact on the ecosystem. This chapter both lauds the splendor of our planet and addresses the urgent environmental problems it faces through colorful descriptions and scientific discoveries. Readers can anticipate interesting stories that stress the need of caring for the environment for future generations and the connection of all life.

Part IV: The Seek of Understanding and Enlightenment
The fourth chapter sets out on a philosophical quest, exploring ideas like knowledge, wisdom, and self-discovery. Through the consideration of literary masterpieces, philosophical texts, and historical sources, this chapter analyzes the eternal quest for understanding the universe, the human mind, and the meaning of life. Encourage reflection and a love of learning with the promise of weighty debates of existentialism, metaphysics, and the transformational power of information.

Concluding Thoughts: A Review of the Trip
The last chapter acts as a reflective endpoint to the literary adventure, allowing readers a chance to examine the issues discussed, the lessons acquired, and the impact of the narratives on their own life. This section summarizes the major points discussed in each chapter, giving the reader an overview of the book's many topics. The final section of the book urges readers to take what they've learned and use it to better themselves and the world around them.

VII. Conclusion and Future Prospects

An examination of how literature, culture, and society will change in the future is provided in the epilogue. This final chapter considers the book's topics and their continued importance, as well as the possible future courses of literature and human thought. By contemplating the future, readers are inspired to contemplate their roles in crafting the narratives of tomorrow, fostering a sense of agency and responsibility in the ever-changing world of ideas and creativity.

Conclusion
Readers who set out on this illuminating literary journey have in store for them a fascinating investigation of interpersonal relationships, societal dynamics, the wonders of nature, and the quest for enlightenment. Each chapter is aimed to give new viewpoints, fascinating anecdotes, and thought-provoking analyses, enabling readers to delve deep into the nuances of the chosen themes. This method of organization ensures that readers will be taken on a journey through a rich tapestry of concepts, feelings, and experiences, making for a book that is both enjoyable and informative. Literature provides a lens through which audiences can examine their own experiences and gain a more nuanced view of the world and their place in it. As the story unfolds, readers are encouraged to see the life-altering influence of literature on their own brains, hearts, and souls.

Chapter 2: The Evolution of Social Media

- **A historical perspective on the development of social media platforms**

    The incredible journey of social media's development demonstrates how technology has changed human contact and communication in profound ways. Social media platforms have evolved from their text-based beginnings to become powerful tools for communication and self-expression in modern society. This essay examines the genesis, important milestones, and revolutionary changes that social media platforms have brought to the digital landscape, providing a detailed historical perspective on their evolution.

    I. The First Social Media Platforms, Pre-Internet
    Bulletin board systems (BBS) and online forums planted the roots of social media long before the internet became a household need. Users of BBS dialed in using modems in the 1970s and 1980s to exchange text-based messages and share files with one another. The spirit of digital connection and collaboration was fostered by these early platforms, which created the groundwork for online communities. At the same time, albeit on a smaller scale, early email systems and Usenet groups allowed for online contact.

    Part Two: The Web 2.0 Revolution and the Rise of New Online Environments
    The introduction of the Internet in the 1990s was a watershed moment in the evolution of social media. Web-based platforms like Six Degrees (1997) allowed users to build profiles and connect with friends, foreshadowing the concept of online social networks. Friendster (2002), however, was the first to popularize the concept of social networking by allowing users to establish profiles, make connections, and share material with others. Following in

Friendster's footsteps are niche social and professional networking sites like MySpace (2003) and LinkedIn (2003).

Expansion of Web 2.0 and Social Media and the Resultant Growth in User-Generated Content

The spread of these many social media platforms may be traced back to the idea of Web 2.0, which emphasizes user-generated content and interactive web experiences. Video sharing was revolutionized by YouTube (2005), which enables users to upload, share, and comment on videos, while photo sharing was made popular by Flickr (2004) among online communities. When it first launched in 2004, Facebook quickly became the most popular social networking site among college students. In 2006, Facebook introduced the News Feed, which prioritized instantaneous updates and social interactions and fundamentally altered the way its users received content.

Topic Four: Real-Time Microblogging Beyond Twitter

In 2006, microblogging systems like Twitter popularized the idea of instantaneous communication via brief messages called tweets. Because of its ease of use and instantaneous nature, Twitter has become a phenomenon all around the world. Concurrently, services like Tumblr (2007) embraced multimedia content, allowing users to share text, photographs, and videos in a blog-like style. Multimedia components were incorporated because they increased user engagement and provided more options for online expression.

Instagram and Snapchat as Visual Storytelling and Instant Reward

The widespread availability of smartphones and advanced mobile cameras has led to the rise of social media sites that emphasize visual content. By enabling users to upload photographs and videos with artistic filters, Instagram (2010) catered to the growing trend of visual storytelling. Its simple design and focus on aesthetics made it extremely widespread, especially among the younger generations. Snapchat (2011) pioneered the concept of ephemeral communications, in which sent images and videos automatically delete themselves after a certain amount of time.

VI. The Rise of Mobile Social Media and the App Economy

With the rapid usage of smartphones and mobile internet, social media networks moved their focus to mobile apps. Social media sites like Facebook, Twitter, and Instagram, as well as many others, have improved their mobile-friendly interfaces to better serve their users. Live broadcasting and Stories, two app-only features, further captivated audiences and prompted spontaneous conversation. Apps for social networking platforms on mobile devices have become indispensable for on-the-go communication and information gathering.

Social Media in Three Dimensions in the Age of VR and AR

Virtual reality (VR) and augmented reality (AR) technology represent the cutting edge of social media innovation. Facebook's Oculus VR (2016) and Microsoft's HoloLens (2016) provide consumers with interactive, social experiences in virtual environments. By fusing digital and physical aspects, augmented reality (AR) applications like Snapchat's AR filters and games like Pokémon Go (2016) increase user engagement and creativity. These innovations represent a paradigm shift, as social media will soon be experienced not just on flat screens, but in full three dimensions.

Conclusion

There has been a remarkable journey of innovation, creativity, and adaptation to societal requirements and technology improvements reflected in the development of social media platforms over time. Social media platforms have continuously developed, influencing how people make connections, share information, and express themselves from the simple text-based interfaces of bulletin board systems to the immersive virtual realities of today.

The future offers even more immersive and interactive social experiences as social media platforms continue to push the frontiers of technology with the incorporation of virtual and augmented realities. Innovative social media platforms that value users' privacy, security, and creative expression have the potential to flourish as a result of the continued development of AI, blockchain technology, and decentralized networks.

Despite the constant upheaval, one thing is certain: social media will continue to be a major factor in how people engage with one another, how they connect with others around the world, and how they tell their own experiences to the world. In the future, it will be crucial to acknowledge the revolutionary potential of social media and its ability to unite people across differences, increase mutual understanding, and honor the rich variety of human experience.

- **Key milestones and innovations in the field**

  Over the course of decades, technology has undergone a remarkable evolution, defined by revolutionary developments and game-changing landmarks that have revolutionized people's everyday lives and professional and social interactions. These watershed moments, ranging from the invention of the wheel to the creation of artificial intelligence, have not only pushed technology forward but also significantly impacted many facets of culture, economy, and society at large. This essay delves at the historical relevance of several technological breakthroughs and developments.

  I. The First Printing Press Is Invented in 1440
  Johannes Gutenberg's development of the printing press in 1440 was one of the most significant advances in technology up to that point. This innovative tool revolutionized the dissemination of knowledge by making books available to a wider audience. The widespread manufacturing of books permitted the transmission of knowledge, leading to the growth of education, scientific discoveries, and cultural interchange. The printing press revolutionized how cultures disseminated information and kept historical records.

  Second, throughout the late 18th and early 19th century, the Industrial Revolution occurred.
  The Industrial Revolution was a watershed moment in human development, ushering in the age of mass production and urbanization through the use of mechanized labor. The steam engine, spinning jenny, and power loom were all significant developments that dramatically improved factory efficiency and output. The advent of factories and assembly lines ushered in a period of economic growth and social advancement. In addition to fostering economic development, the Industrial Revolution also

ushered in profound cultural and social shifts that paved the path for today's industrialized nations.

Incredible progress was made in the fields of communication and transportation throughout the 19th century. Long-distance communication by electrical signals conveyed across wires was made possible by Samuel Morse's creation of the telegraph. This breakthrough completely altered international interaction, making previously inconceivable amounts of time spent communicating across great distances a reality. Concurrently, transcontinental railroads were built, linking once separated areas and easing the transport of commodities, people, and ideas. The advent of both telegraphy and railroads paved the way for global cooperation and integration.

The Telephone (and Its Implications)
The telephone, invented by Alexander Graham Bell in 1876, was a major technological advance in communication. The telephone made it possible to have instantaneous voice contact over great distances, doing away with the necessity for both written communications and in-person meetings. This breakthrough improved interpersonal and organizational communication, leading to new levels of connectivity and productivity. The telephone revolutionized how people, businesses, and governments communicated with one another and helped create a feeling of community.

In the late 20th century, we saw the rise of the Internet and the World Wide Web.
The development of the internet and the World Wide Web in the latter part of the 20th century radically altered the process of gathering and disseminating knowledge. When Tim Berners-Lee developed the World Wide Web in 1989, he made possible a

network of hypertext documents that could be accessed across the web and with one another. This breakthrough simplified worldwide communication, expanded access to multimedia, and democratized knowledge. The proliferation of email, online discussion groups, and social media websites made possible by the internet has fundamentally altered the ways in which people communicate and work together. The internet became a catalyst for digital innovation, leading to the creation of e-commerce, online education, and social media.

Sixth, the 21st century, or the age of mobile devices and smartphones.
The advent of mobile devices and smartphones in the 21st century put the power of computing and the internet into everyone's reach. Smartphones' revolutionary impact on personal computing and communication can be traced back to their introduction of touchscreens, fast CPUs, and internet access. Apps for smartphones and tablets provide a wide variety of useful functions, from location-based services and social networking to media consumption and task management. The widespread adoption of smartphones has resulted in the development of mobile-first strategies across a wide range of fields.

Seventh, the 21st century saw the introduction of artificial intelligence and machine learning.
Artificial intelligence (AI) and machine learning (ML) have come a long way in the 21st century, allowing for the creation of intelligent systems that can learn from data and carry out intricate tasks. Healthcare, finance, transportation, and the arts are just a few of the many industries that have found uses for AI-driven technologies like natural language processing, computer vision, and speech recognition. Machine learning algorithms have enabled predictive analytics, recommendation systems, and autonomous vehicles,

revolutionizing industries and increasing human skills. Technology's future and its possible applications are being shaped by the exponential growth of AI and ML.

Conclusion

The major advances and developments in technology have had a profound effect on society, changing the way people live, work, and learn. Each significant event, from the introduction of the printing press to the development of AI, symbolizes a significant advance in human inventiveness and innovation. These developments have enhanced the lives of billions of people, but they have also brought about new difficulties and ethical questions.

As technology continues to evolve at an unprecedented pace, it is necessary for society to adapt, embrace change, and navigate the evolving digital landscape responsibly. As we move forward, it is essential that we address issues of ethics, privacy, and the fair distribution of technology gains. The transformative potential of innovation can be better appreciated and technology used for the common good when one is familiar with the historical background of significant technical milestones and their impact on society.

- **The role of technology in shaping social media**
    The development of social media and its impact on people's ability to interact with one another and disseminate information are inextricably connected. The development and widespread use of social media in the last few decades have been greatly facilitated by technological developments. This paper investigates the interdependent nature of technology and social media by looking at how various innovations in this field have affected the growth, functionality, and significance of various networking sites.

    I. The Origins of Social Media and Their Roots in Early Technology
    In the early days of the internet, simple online communication tools set the groundwork for what would later become social media. The advent of email systems and online discussion forums heralded the beginning of digital sociability. Online communities and group discussions blossomed with the advent of bulletin board systems (BBS) in the 1970s and 1980s, allowing users to publish messages and share data. These primitive systems paved the way for the growth of advanced social media systems.

    Internet 2.0 and Content Created by Its Users
    The introduction of Web 2.0 in the early 2000s was a watershed moment in the evolution of internet culture. The foundation for contemporary social media was laid in digital 2.0, which is defined by user-generated content and interactive digital experiences. Blogs, wikis, and social networking sites democratized online communication by allowing users to produce, share, and interact on information. Dynamic web interfaces, made possible by technologies like AJAX (Asynchronous JavaScript and XML), increase user engagement and make for a more interesting time spent online. Platforms like Blogger, MySpace, and Friendster encouraged user-generated content, paving the stage for the social media revolution.

Social media's meteoric ascent to prominence, third
The proliferation of social networking sites in the mid-2000s revolutionized methods of making and maintaining connections with others online. Early pioneers included Friendster (2002), LinkedIn (2003), and MySpace (2003), all of which let users build profiles, network with others, and exchange material. Social networking as we know it now was fundamentally altered by Facebook (2004) with the introduction of the News Feed and user timelines. The social networking platform raised the bar with its user-friendly design, multimedia content integration, and constant updates. The popularity of the platform has resulted in a flood of similar sites that are all fighting for users' time and attention.

Accessibility with Mobile Devices and Social Networking Platforms
The development of smartphones and related mobile applications has also contributed to the exponential expansion of social media. Mobile devices with high-speed internet connections and processing capacity have made it possible for people to utilize social media whenever and wherever they like. Instant chatting, photo sharing, and video streaming were just some of the perks that mobile apps brought to users. In order to facilitate content consumption and communication from mobile devices, social media sites streamlined their interfaces. The advent of mobile devices has made social networking an intrinsic part of people's lives, elevating it from its former desktop-only status.

Users' interactions on social media platforms were revolutionized with the introduction of multimedia features like photo and video sharing and live broadcasting. Instagram (2010) and Snapchat (2011) encouraged visual storytelling by facilitating the sharing of photos and videos enhanced by various filters and effects. YouTube (2005) quickly established itself as a central location for online video hosting and consumption. Social media has evolved from a simple means of textual expression to a venue for visual communication thanks to the proliferation of video and other forms of rich media.

Communication via Real Time and Instant Messaging

Real-time communication became a cornerstone of social media platforms, enabling quick interactions and conversations among users. Twitter (2006) popularized microblogging, enabling users to post short, concise messages in real time. The platform's emphasis on concision and real-time made it a global gathering place for the latest developments in news, fashion, and discussion. In real time, users of instant messaging apps like WhatsApp (2009) and Facebook Messenger (2011) may have private or public conversations, share media, and more. Users were able to take part in real-time conversations and global events because to the advent of real-time communication on social media.

Personalized user experiences and content recommendations were made possible by the revolutionary combination of artificial intelligence (AI) and machine learning algorithms on social media platforms. In order to provide relevant content, adverts, and recommendations, AI systems study user behavior, preferences, and interactions. Users can get a more tailored social media experience thanks to personalization algorithms that select content for their feeds, timelines, and suggestions based on their individual preferences. Chatbots powered by AI streamline the customer service process and allow for more meaningful interactions between users. The future of social media platforms and user interactions is being shaped by the ongoing incorporation of AI technologies.

Experiments in Augmented and Virtual Reality

The introduction of AR and VR technologies has brought lifelike experiences to online communities. Filters and effects in augmented reality (AR) apps like Snapchat and Instagram add interactive overlays and animations to users' photographs and videos. Virtual reality (VR) technologies produce synthetic environments in which users can participate in interactive social experiences like online meetings and games. Social media platforms employ AR and VR to boost user engagement, enabling users to explore virtual locations, attend virtual events, and interact with 3D content. New possibilities for human connection and artistic expression are made possible as the line between the virtual and real worlds blurs.

Conclusion

The rise of social media platforms has been inextricably entwined with technology advancements, influencing the way people communicate, share, and connect in the digital age. From the early days of simple online communication to the incorporation of artificial intelligence, augmented reality, and virtual reality, technology has consistently moved the social media revolution forward. Social media has become a dynamic and immersive place thanks to the prevalence of mobile access, the rise of multimedia content, and the ability to tailor one's own experience.

It's expected that as technology develops further, social media sites will include new functions, improve the user interface, and introduce fresh opportunities for users to interact with one another. It is crucial for society to do a critical analysis of the effects of these developments, taking into account things like privacy, digital wellness, and ethical concerns. To successfully navigate the digital landscape and make the most of the potential of social media platforms for good and meaningful connections in the digital age, individuals and communities must first appreciate the mutually beneficial relationship between technology and social media.

- **The growth and diversification of social media users**

    The ways in which individuals create relationships, exchange ideas, and disseminate knowledge have all been revolutionized by the rise of social media platforms. Over the past two decades, these platforms have undergone exponential expansion, transitioning from specialized online communities to large digital landscapes that incorporate different individuals from around the world. This essay investigates the extraordinary increase in social media users, their astonishing diversity, and the mechanisms that have led to this phenomena, as well as its ramifications for global communication, culture, and society.

    Exponential Development: The Surge of Social Media Sites
    Increased internet availability, technological developments, and the widespread availability of smartphones are all significant contributors to the meteoric rise of social media platforms. The social media revolution began in the 2000s with the launch of sites like Friendster, MySpace, and Facebook. The proliferation of social media platforms corresponds to the rise in the availability and accessibility of internet connectivity and mobile devices. Twitter, Instagram, and Snapchat's meteoric rise can be directly attributed to the ease with which their respective apps can be accessed from mobile devices.

    Accessibility of the Internet Around the World
    The widespread availability of internet access has contributed significantly to the rise of social media users. Both developed and developing countries have seen significant increases in Internet penetration rates, making it possible for more people to use social media. With the introduction of 3G, 4G, and now 5G networks, consumers have access to more stable and speedy internet connections, facilitating their smooth usage of social media. In

countries where internet access was limited in the past, initiatives such as Facebook's Internet.org have tried to provide free or affordable internet access, thus extending the user base of social media platforms.

Diversity in the Population: Overcoming Obstacles and Bridging Gaps
As a result of the widespread accessibility of social media, people of all ages, walks of life, and interests may now join the online discourse. Although younger users have predominated on social media sites, the elderly now make up a sizable portion of the user base. The widespread use of sites like Facebook by mature users has changed the conventional wisdom that social media is reserved for the young. People from all walks of life now use social media, making it an indispensable resource for businesses, professions, and politicians.

Differences between Culture and Language
The worldwide accessibility of social media has encouraged the use of multiple languages and cultures online. As a result, people from all over the world can meet one another, learn about one another's cultures, and communicate in their native tongues. Platforms like Twitter and Instagram have enabled users to engage in debates and share content pertaining to their cultural heritage, breaking down cultural boundaries and increasing cross-cultural understanding. As a place where people may interact in their native tongues, social media has also played an important role in preserving linguistic diversity in the modern day.

Influencers and content creators on social media platforms
Diverse user demographics have been attracted thanks in large part to the rise of social media influencers and content creators. Influencers, who have established enormous followings based on

their knowledge, lifestyle, or creativity, appeal to varied audiences, including specialized communities. Users from all walks of life and with all sorts of hobbies are drawn to their content because it hits a chord with them. The proliferation of social media is in large part due to the fact that they feature information that appeals to a wide variety of tastes and interests.

VI. The Power of Social Media to Uplift Underserved Groups in Developing Economies

Social media has given people in underserved communities in developing countries and emerging markets a voice and a place to tell their tales. Social media has been used by activists, NGOs, and grass-roots organizations to educate the public, push for policy reform, and rally support. With the use of social media, groups can now fight stereotypes, demand justice, and have their voices heard on a worldwide scale during social and political movements. As a result of this empowerment, there is now a wider range of stories, viewpoints, and experiences being shared throughout online communities.

The Importance of User-Generated Content in Building Connection and Community

In order to build a sense of community and connection among users, user-generated content (UGC) has become an integral part of social media platforms. By contributing their own stories, images, videos, and commentary, users create a wealth of material that is representative of a wide range of cultures, demographics, and interests. Users of many walks of life can find something in UGC to learn from, be inspired by, and enjoy. The dynamic nature of social media sites encourages users to interact with UGC, leading to more communication and tolerance amongst people with different points of view.

Conclusion

The exponential rise and increasingly varied user base of social media platforms testify to the transformative impact of digital technology in terms of its capacity to break down barriers, forge new alliances, and give a platform to underrepresented groups. Recognizing the significance of openness, digital fluency, and cultural awareness is crucial as social media continue to develop. When people from all walks of life are included in online communities, everyone benefits from a more interesting and dynamic online experience.

In this interconnected digital world, social media facilitates mutual understanding between people of different backgrounds by encouraging them to learn about one another and their experiences. An inclusive and polite online community is essential as society learns to deal with the complexity of the digital age. The full potential of social media as agents of constructive social change, mutual respect, and collective progress in our linked world can be unlocked via an appreciation of users' varied experiences and perspectives.

Chapter 3: Social Media and Cultural Dynamics

- **Exploration of how social media platforms affect cultural trends**

    The emergence of social media platforms has ushered in a new era of communication, information sharing, and cultural exchange. These online communities have evolved into potent instruments that impact and even lead cultural trends in civilizations around the world. The way that cultural trends in everything from fashion and the arts to language and social movements spread and develop has been radically altered by the prevalence and accessibility of social media. This essay delves into the tremendous effect that social media has had on cultural movements, looking at how our views, actions, and identities have been molded by the online communities we frequent.

    I. Global Impact and Rapid Propagation
    The worldwide audience can now be reached instantly by cultural content, trends, and ideas thanks to social media. Cultures that were formerly only known by a small group of people can now go global in a matter of minutes. Visual material may go viral, breaking down barriers of distance and understanding between people everywhere. Through this instantaneous worldwide reach, cultural trends can spread far and wide, influencing the tastes and preferences of a wide variety of people.

    Hybridization and fusion of cultures
    By connecting people from all walks of life and all over the world, social media has paved the way for a mingling of cultures. People can learn about and celebrate the rich diversity of human culture by participating in online communities, forums, and social networking sites. As a result of these interactions, new and exciting hybrid

styles emerge. For example, the blending of traditional clothes with modern fashion trends, such as the global popularity of ethnic-inspired apparel, highlights how social media platforms foster cross-cultural contacts and creativity.

The Role of Content Creators and Influencers in Social Media
Cultural trends are heavily influenced by social media influencers and content creators. These individuals, who have acquired significant followings due to their knowledge, originality, or relatability, have the ability to influence consumer habits and preferences. Many times, influencers team up with brands to promote items and activities that reflect current cultural tendencies. Their carefully selected material and lifestyle choices, shared on platforms like Instagram, YouTube, and TikTok, shape societal norms and ambitions in areas like fashion, beauty, travel, and leisure.

Iterative Trends with Real-Time Data
The instantaneous feedback mechanisms made possible by social media platforms allow users and businesses to rapidly assess the reception of cultural trends. Metrics such as likes, shares, comments, and engagement help determine how well-known and important a trend is. Cultural trendsetters, designers, and content creators may iterate and adjust to audience responses in real time thanks to this real-time feedback loop. Fast iteration in response to user input keeps fads relevant, meaningful, and popular with their intended demographic.

Cultural Stories and Political Change
The cultural narratives and social movements of today have their roots in the social media platforms of yesterday. These online communities provide as a platform for raising awareness and organizing around issues of social justice, identity, diversity, and

inclusion. Awareness may be increased, misconceptions can be confronted, and support for social change can be mobilized through the use of hashtags, viral challenges, and internet campaigns. Movements like #MeToo, #BlackLivesMatter, and #ClimateStrike have gone viral, influencing public opinion, starting conversations, and making a difference in the world.

Definitional Shifts in Verbal Interaction and Expression

New forms of speech, slang, and cybercultures have emerged as a direct result of the rise of social media and its subsequent transformation of how we speak and interact. Platforms like Twitter, with its character limit, have popularized abbreviations, acronyms, and emojis as effective means to transmit emotions and ideas concisely. Memes are a type of cultural expression that have recently gained popularity, especially on social media. Language and cultural expressions are evolving as a result of these digital linguistic trends, which affect both online and offline communication.

While social networking sites help spread new ideas and styles, they also help keep older traditions alive and breathe fresh life into them. Social media platforms provide a platform for indigenous groups, folk artists, craftspeople, and culture vultures to share their heritage, rituals, music, dance, and products with the world. This online exposure aids in the maintenance of cultural customs, piques the interest of people all over the world, and even contributes to economic viability through the selling of traditionally made goods. To preserve cultural diversity and promote cross-cultural appreciation, social media platforms act as digital museums.

Cultural Appropriation and Ethical Considerations

Cultural appropriation ethics are complicated by the quick spread of cultural trends on social media. Misrepresentation or exploitation can result from the inappropriate use of borrowed cultural aspects, behaviors, or artifacts. The rapid dissemination of such examples on social media platforms fuels conflicts and arguments regarding cultural sensitivity, respect, and authenticity. This prompts serious concerns about the ethical application of cultural tendencies and the necessity of cultural education in virtual environments.

- **Case studies on how social media has shaped cultural movements, including fashion, music, and language**

    It is impossible to overestimate the power of social media to influence cultural shifts. Over the past few years, social media platforms have evolved into potent change agents, dramatically altering how individuals experience and participate in many facets of culture, including but not limited to fashion, music, and language. This article examines several examples to show how social media has been instrumental in cultural revolutions, which in turn have brought about profound changes in their respective fields. Through specific instances, we will study the ways in which social media platforms have altered trends, empowered communities, and reshaped cultural narratives.

    I. The Fashion Industry: The Influencer Revolution on Instagram
    The fashion business is one of the most visible examples of a cultural sector that has been significantly impacted by social media. In particular, Instagram has become the go-to site for establishing, debating, and celebrating the latest in the world of fashion. People who have built up a large following and credibility in a particular sector are called "influencers," and they play a crucial role in determining what kinds of clothing will be popular. Fashion influencers have democratized the fashion industry by sharing their personal styles, experimenting with looks, and collaborating with brands to make fashion more approachable and relatable to a wide range of audiences.

    The huge online success of Fashion Nova can be attributed in large part to the company's strategic use of social media influencers. The company teamed up with Instagram celebrities to reach millions of new customers. These public figures, from models to regular people, modeled Fashion Nova's clothes in realistic settings, expanding the brand's potential customer base and broadening its appeal. With the help of Instagram, Fashion Nova launched a community-driven fashion movement that rapidly disseminated and mainstreamed emerging styles.

The Influence of YouTube on the Development of the Music Industry
The emergence of social media platforms, especially YouTube, has caused a seismic upheaval in the music industry. Now more than ever, independent musicians and artists can bypass record labels and get straight to their audiences via online platforms like Twitter and Facebook. As a video-sharing site, YouTube has helped musicians build devoted fan bases and acquire international notoriety by allowing them to upload music videos, live performances, and behind-the-scenes information.

Pop superstar Justin Bieber first became a viral success on YouTube before signing a record deal. Bieber's mother began posting videos of her son's performances on YouTube in 2007. Talent manager Scooter Braun heard him perform his own renditions of well-known songs and was impressed enough to sign him to a record deal, which led to his ultimate rise to fame. Justin Bieber's meteoric rise to fame is a prime example of how platforms like YouTube can help up-and-coming artists break through to the mainstream and have a significant impact on the music industry and the world at large.

Part Three: The Language: How Slang and Memes Have Evolved on Twitter
Twitter in particular has altered the rate of linguistic change and dissemination more than any other social media site. Twitter is perfect for the rapid spread of new words, phrases, and linguistic trends due to the length of tweets and the viral nature of content.

The way we express ourselves, show our feelings, and hold conversations in the digital realm is profoundly influenced by the prevalence of slang, memes, and internet-specific terminology.

Culture on Stan and Twitter: A Case Study
The nickname "Stan," which comes from Eminem's song of the same name, is used to describe an obsessive admirer of a specific celebrity, musician, or television show. On Twitter, where ardent supporters of musicians and actors can be found in droves, the term has taken on new significance. Commonly used slang terminology within internet fandoms include "bias," "fandom," and "ship," all of which have their roots in Stan culture. As an example of how social media platforms like Twitter may alter language and contribute to the growth of online subcultures, stan culture has established a sense of belonging and community among followers through hashtags and trending topics.

The Final Verdict: Social Media's Ongoing Role in Sustaining Cultural Revolutions
This essay uses several examples from the realms of fashion, music, and language to demonstrate how pervasive the impact of social media platforms has become. By making it easier for people to share their ideas and opinions, these platforms have contributed to a more inclusive cultural landscape. With the ever-changing nature of social media comes both opportunities and risks, including but not limited to issues of authenticity, cultural appropriation, and ethical concerns.

Through analysis of these examples, we can better understand the role that social media plays as a catalyst for cultural change. Understanding how to use technology responsibly and having an understanding of other cultures are increasingly important as social media continues to influence social movements. Fostering respectful discussion, appreciating diversity, and encouraging inclusivity are critical steps towards harnessing the positive potential of social media platforms in creating cultural movements for decades to come as individuals and groups negotiate the intricacies of online spaces.

- **The role of influencers and celebrities in cultural shifts**

    Influencers and celebrities have outsized sway over popular sentiment, buying habits, and cultural movements in the modern internet age. These people have broken down barriers and become influential change-makers in their respective fields because of their talent, expertise, or charisma. This essay dives at the many ways in which celebrities and other cultural influencers affect the world around them, including the way we dress, the food we eat, and the opinions we hold.

    I. The Growth of Influencer-Based Societies
    With the advent of social media platforms, it is now easier for anyone with a compelling story, ability, or expertise to gain a significant following. Cultural transformations are increasingly driven by "influencers," or those who have built up significant credibility and authority in their respective fields. People's perceptions of trends and choices have been revolutionized by their capacity to connect with them across demographics, share genuine experiences, and promote items and ideas.

    As trendsetters, fashion influencers create and popularize new looks, aesthetics, and ways of expressing oneself in the industry. Through platforms like Instagram, influencers exhibit their curated looks, combining with fashion brands and designers to create popular campaigns. New fashion movements have emerged as a result of the mutually beneficial interaction between influencers and the fashion industry, which have pushed the boundaries of what constitutes "style."

    Cosmetics and the Beauty Industry
    Influencers have a crucial role in shaping beauty and cosmetics industry trends and consumer preferences. Professional makeup

artists, skincare experts, and beauty vloggers share their knowledge by recommending products, teaching how to use them, and reviewing those they've tried. They influence consumer demand for new cosmetic products and methods with their frank reviews and approachable writing. When influencers team up with cosmetics companies, they often release their own lines of makeup and special edition collections.

Two: Famous People as Icons of Popular Culture

Celebrities, whether from the entertainment, sports, or political sectors, have long been cultural icons, captivating the public's imagination and admiration. They have a significant impact on cultural norms and fashions through the remarks they make and the way of life they lead. Beyond their professional accomplishments, celebrities have an impact through their philanthropy, activism, and social impact projects.

1. Changing Ideals of Beauty

The influence of celebrities in questioning norms of physical attractiveness cannot be overstated. Celebrities have promoted diversity and body positivity by openly celebrating people of all sizes, colors, and forms. Actresses, models, and artists have taken up the cause of self-love and acceptance, helping to change people's ideas about what constitutes beautiful and encouraging them to be proud of who they are.

2. Political and Social Protest

More and more often, famous people speak out about important political and social concerns. People utilize social media to have their voices heard, promote good causes, and fight for social change. Climate change, gender equality, racial justice, and mental health are just some of the topics that have been brought up as a result of their action, which has also influenced public debate and mobilized communities. By using their public profiles to bring attention to social issues and mobilize resources for good causes, celebrities may effect real change.

The ethical problems and challenges brought about by the impact of celebrities and other cultural influencers are substantial. The risks of spreading false information, endorsing unsafe products, and having one's experiences commercialized are all very real worries. The mental health of those who are under constant public scrutiny and are expected to present a carefully crafted online persona is also at risk.

One, Honesty and Accountability
In order to gain their fans' trust, superstars and influencers must always come across as genuine. Authenticity is the defining characteristic of true influencers, as opposed to trend-followers. Ethical influencer marketing necessitates the use of only genuine engagement with followers, openness about sponsored content, and honest product endorsements. Striking a balance between authenticity, brand partnerships, and financial interests is crucial to guaranteeing ethical influence and retaining credibility.

Second, Cyber-Bullying and Emotional Health
Influencers' and celebrities' mental health may suffer as a result of the constant spotlight on their lives. Stress, worry, and emotional anguish can result from being the target of cyberbullying, body shaming, or intrusive media coverage. There has been an uptick in the number of high-profile individuals promoting self-care, open dialogue, and acceptance of mental health issues. Maintaining a healthy and accountable culture of influencers requires attention to mental health issues.

Conclusion

Celebrities and other influential people still play important roles in directing cultural trends and molding public opinion. They have had an effect on social and political activism, body positivity, and mental health advocacy in addition to the fashion and entertainment industries. Authenticity, ethical responsibility, and mental health are crucial when influencers and celebrities face the pressures of the spotlight.

Ethical principles, openness, and a dedication to making the world a better place are necessities in today's climate of influence. By exploiting their platforms properly, influencers and celebrities can contribute to building inclusive, diverse, and sympathetic societal transformations. Understanding the nuances of influence, appreciating authentic voices, and supporting responsible advocacy are all important steps towards harnessing the positive potential of influencer and celebrity culture in shaping a more informed, compassionate, and socially aware society as audiences critically engage with influencers and celebrities.

- **Discussion of the global nature of social media and its impact on cultural diversity**

   In today's globally interconnected digital age, social media has enabled communication across national boundaries and cultural divides. With the advent of social media, people from all over the world are able to connect and share their unique cultures with one another. This essay delves into the tremendous effect that social media has had on cultural variety by looking at how online communities have evolved into thriving ecosystems where different cultures coexist and new ones emerge.

   I. The Role of Culture in the Virtual World
   Social networking sites are like virtual town squares where people of different backgrounds can mingle, exchange stories, and revel in their individuality. Individuals share their ancestry, traditions, and languages with a worldwide audience through photographs, videos, tales, and online discussions. People who have a passion for a particular cultural aspect—be it food, art, music, or language—may find a supportive online community where they can interact with others who share their interests.

   Example: Ethnic Food Blogging and Vlogging
   Cooking lovers and professionals from a variety of cultural backgrounds frequently start blogs and YouTube channels with the express purpose of disseminating regionally specific recipes and methods of preparation. These spaces not only encourage people from different backgrounds to interact with one another, but also teach people all around the world about different cuisines, ingredients, and cooking techniques. These creators make the Internet a cultural melting pot by sharing recipes from all over the world and using visually appealing content to do it.

   The Languages Spoken Around the World

The use of social media has helped to preserve and spread linguistic diversity. Bridging the gap between oral histories and the modern digital age, people are now better equipped than ever to communicate in their original languages. Twitter, Facebook, and Instagram users regularly engage in conversations with one another in which different languages and idiomatic idioms are used.

Example: Using Social Media to Promote Indigenous Language Revitalization
Indigenous peoples all across the world are using the internet and mobile phones to save their languages from extinction. Members of the community work together to develop language-learning resources, exchange oral stories, and host virtual language lessons using mediums such as Facebook groups, YouTube channels, and Twitter accounts. The global reach of social media is helping to preserve indigenous languages and encouraging new generations to learn about and appreciate their heritage.

Thirdly, Cultural Education and Awareness
With the use of social media, we can learn about other cultures, eliminate prejudice, and increase understanding among people of different backgrounds. Museums, galleries, and universities all use online platforms to disseminate information about their collections and programs to people all over the world. Live broadcasts, VR experiences, and digital displays help people all over the world learn about and appreciate one another's cultures and customs.

The museum and heritage sector has embraced social media in order to provide virtual tours and user-generated content. Museums promote cultural awareness and education by making their collections available to a worldwide audience through high-quality pictures, 360-degree movies, and live Q&A sessions. To ensure that cultural history is not lost to future generations, social media platforms act as digital archives.

IV. International Cooperation and the Merging of Cultures

Artists, musicians, writers, and innovators from all over the world may work together on projects and reach a wider audience thanks to the reach of social media. Artworks, music, literature, and fashion all benefit from the fusion of cultural components when people from different backgrounds work together.

Fusion genres and cross-cultural collaborations in music: a case study

Across continents, musicians and artists of varying cultural origins work together to create new works that fuse traditional and modern sounds, styles, and techniques. Platforms like YouTube and SoundCloud allow musicians to publish their collaborative work, introducing worldwide audiences to fusion music styles that merge different traditions smoothly. These kind of projects not only celebrate cultural variety but also encourage people to value new forms of artistic expression.

Concerns and Issues Related to Maintaining Cultural Authenticity

The cultural authenticity and appropriation issues are exacerbated by the fact that social media platforms celebrate cultural diversity. Concerns concerning the monetization of cultural practices, symbols, and artifacts have been raised due to the blurring of lines between appreciation and appropriation in the digital environment. Sharing cultural components, especially those that are considered sacred or delicate, requires a special level of sensitivity and care.

Conclusion

The interconnectedness of the world has made the Internet a rich tapestry of languages, customs, and civilizations. People all over the world are having conversations on social media that highlight and honor our shared humanity. Understanding one another's cultures, learning new languages, and working together across borders are all facilitated by social media.

It is essential to approach online interactions with sensitivity, respect, and cultural knowledge if we want to maximize the good impact of social media on cultural diversity. Social media can play an important role in promoting cultural interchange, mutual respect, and global solidarity if its users continue to learn from one another's experiences and opinions and share their own. Our shared human experience is enriched and our connections across borders and continents are strengthened when we embrace the worldwide tapestry of cultures displayed on social media platforms as we move through the digital world.

Chapter 4: The Influence of Social Media on Identity and Self-Expression

- **Examination of how social media platforms impact individual and group identities**

    How people see themselves and how they interact with the world around them has been profoundly altered by the prevalence of social media. Individuals can create a distinct online character and find groups of people who share their interests in these virtual environments. At the same time that it shapes communal narratives and promotes unity across disparate communities, social media also affects individual identities. This essay delves into the complex ways in which online communities like Facebook, Twitter, and Instagram affect our sense of ourselves, our relationships with others, and the groups we belong to as a whole.

    I. How People Form Their Own Unique Selves
    Making a Good Impression in the Digital Age
    People might use social media to present an idealized image of themselves, one that highlights only the qualities they deem most important or interesting. Individuals provide a controlled digital identity that reflects their preferred image through carefully selected images, status updates, and shared content. This method of self-presentation facilitates introspection by offering a forum for articulating and testing out various aspects of one's identity.

    Self-esteem and body image issues have been linked to the proliferation of picture-centric social media platforms like Instagram and Snapchat. Particularly among young users, making comparisons to idealized images might result in feelings of inadequacy and low self-esteem. Social media platforms often contribute to the establishment of beauty standards, impacting users' judgments of attractiveness and self-worth. They also serve as platforms for self-affirmation and the rejection of conventional beauty standards, so promoting a broader and more accepting concept of one's own identity.

Group identities and the role of social media
Creating Space for Groups and Movements

Communities and subcultures bound by common interests, hobbies, and worldviews flourish on social media platforms. Whether it's through fandoms, online gaming groups, or social justice campaigns, people are able to connect with others who share their interests and values. These online communities allow people to come together online and share their interests, find people who can relate to them, and build stronger group identities through shared experiences and activities.

Insular groups and ideological divisions

Although social media sites let people connect with one another, they also have the potential to isolate users by exposing them only to material and arguments that confirm their own worldviews. This phenomena has the potential to exacerbate existing prejudices and polarize society discussions, fostering the development of competing group identities. The echo chamber effect can exacerbate tensions within communities by stifling open communication and mutual understanding.

Identity Presentation and Interpersonal Dynamics
Authenticity in a Digital Environment

Individuals can put on a show of who they are on social media, exhibiting characteristics, values, and perspectives that might not reflect their true selves. The authenticity of online interactions is called into doubt when a person's real life and their digital self become entangled in a performance. The tailored online personae that many people present to the world can be difficult to distinguish from their real-life counterparts thanks to the performative aspect of social media.

Effects on Social Interactions

The dynamics of people's connections with one another are molded by the ways in which they use social media. Social media sites make it possible for people to keep in touch with one another, share news and experiences, and socialize regardless of physical proximity. Relationships might suffer when people use these sites for meaningless activities like social comparison, jealously, and miscommunication. In addition, people's perceptions of one another and their interpretation of social cues may be impacted because of the lack of nuance in online interactions compared to in-person encounters.

Social media platforms have become forums where individuals can explore and express their intersectional identities, embracing the nuances of their lived experiences. The interconnectedness of social categories such as race, gender, sexual orientation, and socioeconomic status is emphasized in online communities. Those on the margins can use these venues to get their voices heard, push for positive social change, and question entrenched injustices. However, they also emphasize the issues encountered by marginalized individuals online, since they put users at risk of harassment, hate speech, and discrimination based on many parts of their intersecting identities.

Conclusioz

It's no secret that the rise of social media has had a profound effect on how people see themselves and how they interact with others. There are both positive and bad effects of social media on one's sense of self. While these channels allow users to learn more about themselves, make new friends, and speak out on issues that matter to them, they may also wreak havoc on confidence, honesty, and interpersonal bonds.

Understanding how social media shapes individuals and communities is crucial for success in the online world. The beneficial potential of social media can only be unlocked through the widespread adoption of digital literacy, the promotion of empathy, and the encouragement of courteous online interactions. An inclusive and empathetic society can be fostered in both the online and offline worlds by fostering an online environment where diverse identities are respected, celebrated, and understood. This can be achieved by recognizing the complexities of identity performance, understanding the nuances of group dynamics, and advocating for inclusive online spaces.

- **Analysis of the impact on self-esteem and self-perception**

  To express ourselves, make new friends, and disseminate information, social media sites have become indispensable in the modern digital world. Despite their usefulness, social media have also been linked to a number of troubling psychological effects. Their influence on individuals' senses of worth and identity is a major source of worry. This essay explores into the various ways in which social media affects people's sense of self-worth and identity, discussing both the positive and bad effects of this phenomenon online.

  I. Reflection in the Virtual Mirror (Social Media)
  Analyzing Human Interactions Side by Side
  Many people use social media as a place to look at others and judge them based on their own standards of success and attractiveness. The selective nature of the content presented on these platforms has been linked to the development of inflated senses of self-importance and inferiority. Constant exposure to others' meticulously created photos and posts might distort one's perspective of reality, leading them to doubt their own value and abilities.

  Acceptance and Praise from Others
  Self-esteem can be negatively affected by the constant need for social media "approval" in the form of likes, comments, and shares. A sense of societal approbation, like that provided by compliments, can do wonders for a person's sense of self-worth and confidence. On the other hand, a lack of likes or negative feedback might have the opposite impact, leaving you feeling rejected and uncertain of your own abilities. The reliance on external validation from social media interactions might damage individuals' intrinsic self-esteem,

making them subject to changes in their self-worth based on online comments.

Standards of Ideal Beauty

Idealized beauty standards are frequently promoted on social media, with a focus on certain body shapes, skin tones, and other physical features. Younger users, in particular, are vulnerable to the negative effects of being exposed to these idealized images, which might include body dissatisfaction and low self-esteem. Individuals' impressions of their own bodies and appearances can be affected by the continual comparison to digitally manipulated photos.

The World Is Filtered With Them

Users are able to display an idealized picture of themselves on social media due to the popularity of image-enhancing filters and editing tools. These instruments have the potential to be entertaining and imaginative, but they also have the capability of distorting one's own sense of reality. People can become attached to the filtered versions of themselves and become unhappy with their natural appearance. Self-esteem and body image can be negatively affected when an individual's online identity does not match their actual life.

III. The Upside: Independence and Encouragement

Communities That Care

Despite the difficulties, social media still provides places where people may connect with like-minded people and feel safe to express their feelings. There is comfort and strength to be found in the many online communities that focus on mental health, body positivity, and self-acceptance. These communities provide a sense of belonging, acceptance, and understanding, providing individuals with the fortitude to fight society pressures and develop positive self-perception.

Liberation and the Freedom to Be Oneself

People are able to share their individuality, interests, and skills on social networking sites. Social media provides a space for people from underrepresented groups to dispel myths, encourage inclusion, and celebrate individuality. Individuals can strengthen their sense of identity and self-worth by honest self-expression, which in turn helps them view themselves favorably and better withstand the negative effects of peer pressure.

Skillful Use of Social Media: Finding Your Way in the Cyberworld

Ability to Think Analytically and Digitally

In order to help people properly traverse the digital landscape, it is crucial to promote digital literacy and critical thinking abilities. Social media users can be prepared to engage with a more critical perspective if they have been taught to distinguish between curated online information and real-world experiences. Users can participate more thoughtfully when they have an understanding of the psychology behind social media algorithms and the effect of online validation.

Building Good Online Routines

Promoting positive online behavior is important for people's sense of identity and self-worth. The negative effects of frequent exposure can be lessened by instituting limits, taking pauses, and avoiding excessive comparison to one's own or others' online lives. More meaningful and helpful conversations can be sparked when users are encouraged to put less emphasis on seeking approval and more on making actual connections.

Conclusion

Self-esteem and self-perception are affected by a number of elements, both positive and negative, when using social media. Though social media can be used to express oneself, make new friends, and gain confidence, it also comes with risks such as social comparison, unattainable beauty standards, and the need for external validation. It's crucial to recognize the paradox of the digital age, when social media can both boost confidence and erode it.

The digital landscape can be navigated with resilience and confidence if we teach people how to use technology effectively, help them accept themselves as they are, and encourage them to use social media in a conscious way. Individuals can benefit from social media while protecting their sense of self-worth and confidence by practicing self-compassion and cultivating true connections with others and with themselves. Maintaining a positive identity in the digital age requires cultivating a healthy relationship with social media, which continues to affect our interactions and sense of self.

- ## The concept of "digital selves" and the implications for personal branding

    There is a new notion in the world thanks to the proliferation of digital technology and the impact of social media: the "digital self." In today's highly linked world, people's online personas are typically carefully crafted to represent their goals, passions, and core beliefs. This "digital self," as it is sometimes called, has far-reaching consequences for one's personal brand and also affects how they are seen online. This essay delves into the idea of "digital selves," taking a close look at their construction, their effect on personal branding, and the potential and threats they pose in today's online world.

    I. Creating Online Personas: Carefully Crafted Personas in Cyberspace
    Identity Management and Social Media
    Social media platforms serve as the major forums where individuals craft their digital selves. Users present pieces of their lives through carefully selected posts, photographs, and interactions, crafting digital narratives that speak to their passions, accomplishments, and experiences. These sites provide outlets for individuality, letting users modify their online personas to better suit their needs in life and work.

    Authenticity and Performance
    There is frequently a fine line between being oneself online and performing for an audience. People's online identities can be shaped using a combination of actual and fabricated content in an effort to attract positive attention and advance their careers. Finding this sweet spot is essential for successful personal branding, since being genuine builds trust and credibility while appearing fake can have the opposite effect.

    Making Your Online Identity II: The Digital You and Personal Branding
    Consistency with Objectives for One's Own Brand
    The concept of digital identities connects closely with personal branding, the deliberate attempt to change how one is viewed by others. People frequently utilize social media to bolster their personal brand, adapting their online identities to reflect their ideal professional or personal representation. A unified personal brand that resonates with the target audience requires consistency in language, images, and values across digital channels.

    The online persona can serve as a potent medium for demonstrating credibility and mastery in a given topic. Individuals can establish themselves as industry leaders by publishing insightful articles, videos, and other internet material. By participating in discussions and sharing one's successes on social media, one might further establish him or herself as an authority figure online.

III. Obstacles and Moral Concerns

Personal Space and Limits

Keeping your digital identity separate from your private data might be difficult. In the same way that being too guarded might prevent genuine interactions, exposing too much personal information can lead to unwanted intrusions. In order to safeguard one's privacy and keep one's digital self feeling genuine, one must establish clear boundaries and be cautious of the information given online.

Controlling Your Digital Image

Problems in maintaining a positive online identity are a real threat to the digital self. Personal branding initiatives might take a serious hit in the event of negative reviews, internet criticism, or provocative utterances. Essential abilities for thriving in today's connected world include the ability to respond maturely to criticism, show empathy for others' perspectives, and take charge of one's online reputation.

Possibilities and Prospective Developments

Making Content and Telling Tales Online

The digital you relies heavily on your ability to create content and deliver stories in digital form. People can communicate interesting stories, impart knowledge, and interact with their audience by using multimedia forms including blogs, podcasts, videos, and social media posts. In order to build a great personal brand, it's important to convey stories that are true to yourself online.

Adopting New Technological Developments

Virtual reality (VR) and augmented reality (AR) are two examples of cutting-edge tech that can be used to improve one's online identity and reputation. Immersive virtual reality (VR) platforms make it possible for individuals to hold virtual events, seminars, or conferences, while augmented reality (AR) applications improve interactive marketing and engagement techniques. Adopting these innovations can help the digital persona soar, resulting in engaging and original content.

Conclusion

The idea of a "digital self" has revolutionized the way people interact with and build their reputations in the digital world. There are advantages and disadvantages that come along with the growing trend of people curating their digital personas on social media. A careful balancing act between personal expression, professionalism, and ethical considerations is required to craft an authentic, consistent, and compelling digital self.

Individuals may better their digital selves and their personal brands by embracing the power of storytelling, utilizing multimedia forms, and adapting to changing technologies. However, it is necessary to remain cognizant of privacy, ethical boundaries, and online reputation management. Constant introspection, flexibility, and an in-depth knowledge of the ever-changing digital landscape are required for success in navigating the junction of digital identities and personal brands. To make meaningful connections, establish powerful personal brands, and leave an indelible mark in the digital age, individuals must continue to craft their digital selves.

- **Consideration of the positives and negatives of social media in terms of self-expression**

  The proliferation of social media has changed the way people share their thoughts and ideas forever by providing new venues for self-expression, interpersonal communication, and introspection. There are advantages to expressing oneself in the digital sphere, but there are also risks associated with doing so. This essay delves into the tangled web of social media and individual expression, weighing the pros and cons of both as experienced by modern internet users.

  I. The Upsides of Social Media for Personal Expression
  Expression of Talent and Self-Reliance
  Individuals are able to openly share their views, feelings, and talents on social media sites, making them potent creative avenues. Users can share their originality, skill, and insight in the form of video, photography, and text. Sharing one's interests, talents, and creations with people all over the world is made possible by social media and can lead to feelings of pride and satisfaction.

  Strengthening Ties Within Communities
  Communities of people who share common goals, values, and experiences are easier to establish thanks to the widespread availability of social media. People of all walks of life can find each other and form communities based on mutual respect and an appreciation for unique perspectives. People's sense of community and self-worth can be improved by their participation in online forums, groups, and social media pages, where they can talk freely about their passions and experiences with like-minded people and receive positive reinforcement for doing so.

  Boosting Community Action and Expression
  The voices of the underrepresented have been amplified and advocacy campaigns have been given a boost thanks to the

proliferation of social media platforms. It is possible for people to bring attention to social problems, disprove prejudices, and push for constructive change. Social justice can be advanced through the use of hashtags, viral campaigns, and internet petitions, which bring people together around shared values and allow for more freedom of expression.

The Downsides of Social Media Self-Expression

Feelings of Inadequacy and Social Comparison

One of the main negatives of social media is the culture of comparison it generates. Inadequacy and low self-esteem might result from constantly being exposed to curated, idealized images of other people's life. A person's sense of self-worth could suffer if they compare their situation to that of another. The fear of being judged negatively by others online might lead to a suppression of one's true feelings.

Assaults on the Cyberspace and the Web

Cyberbullying and online harassment, in which victims are anonymously targeted, criticized, or threatened over social media, are a growing problem. When people's self-worth and confidence are damaged in this way, they become less likely to speak their minds. Incidents of cyberbullying can cause victims mental discomfort, worry, and isolation, all of which inhibit the development of one's full creative potential.

Self-Deception Caused by Filtering

Image-enhancing filters and editing tools that are so widely available on social networking sites can affect how people feel about their bodies. A person's online and offline identities may become increasingly disjointed if they believe they must offer an idealized image of themselves. The pressure to look a certain way online can lead to the promotion of unhealthy ideals of beauty, which in turn can have negative effects on self-esteem and the freedom to express oneself creatively in terms of one's physical appearance.

III. Methods for Balancing Contradictions in Expressing Oneself Healthily

Ability to Think Analytically and Digitally

It is crucial to help people understand the intricacies of social media by promoting digital literacy and critical thinking abilities. Users can gain the ability to critically engage with social media by learning about the impact of algorithms, the psychology of online interactions, and the significance of curated material. Developing critical thinking abilities enables users to differentiate between true self-expression and idealized digital personas, enabling a better engagement with social media.

Fostering Self-Care and Emotional Toughness

Encouraging self-compassion and emotional resilience can help individuals cope with the problems of social media. Self-compassion is the practice of being kind and understanding to oneself, especially while facing criticism or comparisons about oneself online. Emotional resilience is the ability to recover quickly from setbacks, which is essential for maintaining one's own unique voice in the face of online adversity.

Meditation and putting down the phone

To foster awareness of one's online interactions and emotional responses, it's important to encourage "mindful engagement" with social media. By establishing limits, scheduling regular "digital detoxes," and being cognizant of the effects of social media on one's mental and emotional health, one can develop a more positive perspective on expressing oneself online. Maintaining a healthy sense of self-worth and genuine expression calls for a balance between online and offline activities.

Conclusion

Every day, people must negotiate the shifting terrain created by the pros and cons of self-expression on social media. Understanding the benefits and drawbacks of online expression is crucial for developing a positive perspective on social media. Individuals can take use of the benefits of social media while protecting their sense of self-worth and freedom of expression by fostering digital literacy, cultivating self-compassion, and encouraging thoughtful interaction.

A delicate equilibrium of originality, honesty, and emotional fortitude is required for successful self-expression in the modern digital age. Individuals can nurture a sense of self-worth and fulfillment in the digital sphere by cultivating an authentic and empowered online presence that acknowledges and capitalizes on the positives and employs techniques to resolve the downsides. Understanding the yin and yang of this digital landscape is essential for navigating the complexity of the modern, interconnected world as people continue to explore the immense possibilities of self-expression on social media.

Chapter 5: The Implications for Society and Policy

- **Discussion of the societal consequences of the widespread use of social media**

    The proliferation of social media has altered the very nature of human interaction, altering the ways in which individuals build communities, share information, and make sense of the world around them. While social media platforms offer several benefits, such as increased communication and worldwide connectivity, they also bring forth a plethora of societal consequences. This essay explores the far-reaching effects of social media, looking at its benefits and its drawbacks for individuals, groups, and organizations.

    International Cooperation and Communcation
    Because of social media, people from all over the world are able to communicate and work together in real time regardless of their location. Connecting people from all over the world and allowing them to exchange information and work together on projects is a great way to promote mutual understanding and cooperation among nations. This increased connectedness has aided global movements by bringing together activists, academics, and organizations to work towards goals that transcend boundaries.

    Action and Mobilization in the Social World
    Individuals and groups can now more easily organize and take action for social change with the help of social media. Social media has been instrumental in the growth of movements like #MeToo, Black Lives Matter, and environmental activism, all of which aim to educate the public about social injustices and alter public discourse. These online movements questioned established norms, which

sparked in-person conversations about larger systemic problems and motivated people to take action.

II. Obstacles to Emotional and Psychological Well-Being

Problems with Self-Esteem and Comparing to Others

The influence of social media on mental health is one of the medium's most far-reaching social effects. Social comparison, in which people evaluate their own worth based on the depictions of others online, can be a negative effect of constantly being exposed to curated information and glorified lifestyles. Especially among young users who are more vulnerable to the pressures of online validation, this tendency can lead to feelings of inadequacy, low self-esteem, and anxiety.

Assaults on the Cyberspace and the Web

Cyberbullying and online harassment are on the rise, and the anonymity given by social media platforms may encourage their use. Victims of internet abuse may experience emotional discomfort, sadness, and social disengagement. Concerns about the long-term psychological effects of cyberbullying episodes, particularly among adolescents, have prompted the development of comprehensive online safety measures and digital literacy initiatives.

Quick Dissemination of News

The advent of social media platforms has radically altered the rate at which information may be disseminated. During times of crisis, communities can stay aware and prepared with the help of real-time information shared on social media. Rapid information sharing via social media has also been essential in bringing attention to global issues, such as climate change, public health, and social justice.

Problems with False Information and Media Coverage

However, the rapid dissemination of false information has been made possible by the accessibility and efficiency of social media platforms. The public's trust in authoritative institutions can be eroded when false information, conspiracy theories, and disinformation efforts get widespread attention. To combat the spread of false information, people need to learn how to evaluate sources critically and be educated in media literacy. Additionally, platforms, governments, and civil society must work together.

IV. Digital Surveillance and Privacy Concerns

Erosion of Privacy

Significant privacy concerns are raised by social media companies' gathering and processing of user data. Individuals' privacy is compromised when sensitive information is shared online and then utilized for purposes such as targeted advertising, spying, and data mining. Concerns regarding the abuse of personal information and the weakening of privacy protections arise frequently as a result of the tracking of users' online activities, preferences, and interactions.

Controlling Society Through Technology and Big Data

Social media platforms have becoming increasingly used by governments and agencies for digital monitoring and social control. Surveillance methods, such as monitoring internet communications and tracking activists, raise issues about privacy rights and freedom of expression. Digital monitoring can stifle dissent, limit freedom of speech, and infringe upon individuals' rights to privacy, posing serious problems to democratic society.

Cultural Change and Social Media

Sharing one's own culture, language, and customs with an international audience is made easier by the proliferation of social media platforms. Cross-cultural understanding is encouraged and varied viewpoints are celebrated in online groups that focus on specific cultural interests. The importance of social media in bridging generational gaps and maintaining cultural identities in the modern digital age is growing.

Cultural sensitivity and appropriation

However, the worldwide reach of social media also brings up questions of cultural insensitivity and appropriation. Misrepresentations and commercialization of cultural components including clothing, language, and symbols can foster cultural insensitivity and keep harmful stereotypes alive. By sparking conversations about cultural sensitivity and respect for other traditions, social media can help bring attention to the problem of cultural appropriation.

Conclusion

Social media's widespread adoption marked the beginning of a new era of global communication and cultural understanding. These platforms provide revolutionary chances for societal advancement, but they also present formidable problems that need careful consideration. Critical steps in negotiating the complicated landscape of social media's societal repercussions include addressing mental health concerns, combatting disinformation, ensuring privacy, and encouraging cultural awareness.

The importance of encouraging digital literacy, ethical online behavior, and civil conversation is growing as people try to make sense of the long-term effects of social media on our culture. Harnessing the beneficial potential of social media while reducing its bad influence requires collaborative efforts by platforms, governments, schools, and users. It is possible for society to build a digital environment that promotes positive social change, inclusivity, and informed debate by encouraging responsible usage and creating a culture of empathy and understanding online.

- **Exploration of issues related to privacy, misinformation, and cyberbullying**

    Privacy concerns, false information, and cyberbullying are three of the most pressing problems that the digital landscape, and especially the world of social media, has presented to society. Examining the effects on individuals, groups, and society as a whole, this essay looks into the complex web of issues concerning privacy, misinformation, and cyberbullying in the digital era.

    Confidentiality Online, Part I
    Information Gathering and Monitoring
    Data collection and analysis have reached new heights thanks to the popularity of social media. Concerns about privacy erosion are prompted by the precise tracking of individuals' personal information, preferences, and online habits. Companies employ this data for targeted advertising, often blurring the line between tailored marketing and intrusion into individuals' private life. Concerns regarding digital privacy have been raised in response to the constant monitoring, highlighting the importance of open data policies and strict privacy laws.

    Identity Theft and Online Safety
    Online security risks abound in today's interconnected digital world. Cybercriminals use weaknesses to participate in identity theft, phishing attacks, and fraud, risking individuals' financial and personal information. While social media sites bring people together, they can also be a haven for criminal activity, therefore it's important that users understand the value of using a strong, unique password to protect their accounts.

    Misinformation, Part II: A Persistent Problem
    Rapid Propagation of Misinformation

The quick spread of both true and misleading news throughout the internet and social media is a consequence of the digital age. Sensationalist news, conspiracy theories, and edited content are common ways that false information can become viral, reaching millions of people in a matter of minutes. The rapid spread of false information poses a threat to the veracity of data, distorts people's views of the world, and erodes faith in reputable news outlets.

Taking on the Problem of False Information
Defeating disinformation calls for a multipronged strategy. The ability to examine information sources critically and distinguish between reliable news and misinformation is greatly aided by media literacy education. By adding fact-checking processes, encouraging accurate material, and penalizing accounts that propagate misleading information, social media platforms can play a significant role in reducing the spread of disinformation. The impact of false information on society can only be reduced by joint efforts between platforms, fact checkers, and educators.

The Unsavory Side of Online Interactions (III) Cyberbullying
The Emotional Cost of Cyberbullying
The problem of cyberbullying, in which people use the Internet to harass, intimidate, or humiliate others, has become pervasive, especially among younger users. Cyberbullying victims go through emotional turmoil, worry, and loneliness. The anonymity of the internet gives abusers confidence, making it harder for victims to confront their tormentors. Incidents of cyberbullying can have devastating results, including damage to a person's mental health or even suicide.

Help and Safety Measures
Individuals, institutions, families, and online communities must all work together to combat cyberbullying. Instilling empathy and

discouraging cyberbullying are two outcomes of education programs that emphasize digital ethics and courteous online behavior. When it comes to cyberbullying, it's important for schools and parents to take preventative measures. In order to make the internet a safer place, social media sites should have comprehensive reporting procedures and take immediate action against offenders.

Conclusion

Individuals and society alike face serious issues in the digital age, including privacy worries, false information, and cyberbullying. Policymakers, IT corporations, schools, parents, and users must all work together to find solutions to these problems. Maintaining a welcoming and safe online community for all users requires a balance between free speech and responsible behavior.

Critically navigating the digital realm is made easier with knowledge about online safety, media literacy, and digital ethics. Websites like Facebook and Twitter need to keep spending money on tools and regulations that protect their users' privacy and ensure they are provided with correct information. Creating a culture where online interactions are polite and inclusive requires communities to build empathy, understanding, and support.

Society may take use of the benefits of digital platforms while minimizing their drawbacks if its members recognize the risks posed by issues like privacy invasion, false information, and cyberbullying and work together to combat them. If we want to live in a digital environment where our personal information is protected, where news is reliable, and where our interactions with others online are safe, we must teach people how to use technology responsibly, instill in them a sense of digital citizenship, and encourage ethical online behavior.

- **Analysis of government and industry responses and regulations**

The internet and social media have changed the way civilizations work because of how quickly they have developed and spread. With this digital transformation comes a plethora of difficulties, ranging from privacy concerns and cybersecurity threats to misinformation and online harassment. Regulatory measures and industry-led initiatives have been implemented in response to these problems on a global scale. This article evaluates the responses of governments and companies to the difficulties of the digital age, evaluating the efficiency of legislation and the shifting landscape of digital governance.

I. Official Reactions and Rules

Privacy and Data Security Legislation

As the need to protect individuals' privacy has become more apparent, many countries have passed data protection legislation. One such regulation that establishes stringent guidelines for the collection, processing, and storage of personal data is the General Data Protection Regulation (GDPR) of the European Union. These rules give people more say over their personal data and make businesses more accountable for protecting it.

Rules for Internet Safety

The importance of cybersecurity in the modern digital era has been widely acknowledged by governments around the world. Protecting vital infrastructure, sensitive government data, and individuals' information is a primary goal of cybersecurity rules and standards. Governments work with cybersecurity professionals and groups to develop policies and procedures for protecting information networks, thwarting attacks, and recovering from hacks.

Regulation of Content and Security in Cyberspace

Governments have begun to address the issue of content moderation on social media platforms due to the proliferation of dangerous content, misinformation, and online harassment. Governments have been working on legislation that hold platforms accountable for content uploaded on their sites, while it is difficult to strike a balance between free speech and the need to safeguard users from harmful content. In order to create a less dangerous virtual space, users count on social media platforms to invest in content moderation tools and act swiftly in response to reports of harmful user conduct.

Programs to Promote Digital Literacy in the Classroom
To help individuals, especially young people, learn to use the internet safely and responsibly, many governments have implemented digital literacy and online safety initiatives. Cybersecurity, fake news, good netiquette, and the need for careful thought when using the internet are all topics that these campaigns hope to address. Governments can help citizens stay safe from cybercriminals and make educated choices in the digital sphere by encouraging the spread of digital literacy.

Sectoral Reactions and Self-Regulatory Practices
Guidelines for Social Media Platforms
To reduce the spread of dangerous content, hate speech, and disinformation, social media platforms have developed community guidelines and content moderation procedures. While platforms are attempting to self-regulate, it can be difficult to enforce rules uniformly among millions of users. Maintaining an upper hand against ever-evolving online threats requires constant changes to algorithms, AI, and human moderation teams.

Working Together with Those Who Check Their Facts

In order to combat the spread of false information, social media sites have teamed up with watchdog groups that verify claims made online. These partnerships strive to identify trustworthy material from incorrect or misleading content, providing consumers with proper context and helping them to make informed decisions. Fact-checking activities help the fight against misinformation, yet obstacles remain, such as the speed at which misinformation spreads.

Accountability Reports and Openness to the Public
In an effort to be more open and honest, tech companies have begun publishing transparency reports that include data on the frequency of material removals, government demands for user data, and measures taken against accounts that violate platform regulations. Users are better able to evaluate how platforms moderate content and handle user data when transparency measures are in place. The reports' adequacy and the level of transparency given, however, continue to raise questions.

Third, Issues and Future Thoughts
International Harmonization and Consensus
Given the global nature of the digital landscape, international collaboration is crucial for tackling issues like cybersecurity threats and cross-border data flows. Sharing best practices, harmonizing rules, and working together to combat cybercrime are all made possible through international collaboration. By harmonizing data protection and content moderation regulations, for example, we may establish a single foundation for digital governance on a global scale.

Striking a Balance between Rules and New Ideas
It's important to strike a balance when regulating digital platforms so as not to restrict innovation and economic growth. Nuanced laws

that encourage innovation while assuring ethical and responsible behaviors are necessary to strike the correct balance between safeguarding users and fostering technology breakthroughs. The regulatory frameworks put in place must be adaptable so that they can keep up with the dynamic nature of the digital world.

Promoting User Agency and Computer Literacy

The key to creating a secure digital space is educating individuals and improving their digital literacy. Governments and businesses should fund programs that instruct people, especially young people, in the skills of critical thinking, media literacy, and online safety. Users who take the time to educate themselves are better able to spot false information, safeguard their privacy, and use digital platforms safely and ethically.

Conclusion

Governments and businesses alike must respond carefully to the unprecedented opportunities and problems that the digital age has brought forth. A complete approach for navigating the intricacies of the digital frontier must include effective legislation, collaborative efforts, transparency, and digital literacy initiatives. Societies may take advantage of technology's benefits while minimizing its drawbacks through more international cooperation, a healthy dose of regulation, and user education and empowerment.

- **A look at potential future policies and regulations to address social media's impact on society**

    Regulating social media platforms to limit their negative impact while preserving the benefits of digital connectedness and expression is a challenging task for governments throughout the world as social media continues to permeate every area of modern society. The future of social media is discussed in this essay, along with the policies and regulations that could shape it. Topics covered include privacy, fake news, cyberbullying, and the societal impact of social media. Governments may create a more secure and welcoming online space for all citizens by considering novel ideas.

I. Data Security and Privacy Protection

Strong, All-encompassing Privacy Laws

The implementation of strict data protection legislation, like the General Data Protection Regulation (GDPR), should be a top priority for future policies. Users' rights to privacy, data portability, and erasure must all be protected by these statutes. Companies need to be held accountable for being open about their data gathering techniques and granting users fine-grained access to their data. Platforms will be encouraged to protect user privacy if they face severe consequences for not doing so.

Ability to Move and Share Data

Users would be able to switch between services without losing any of their data if social media platforms encouraged data portability and interoperability. This method promotes healthy competition and discourages monopolistic behavior, giving consumers the freedom to select platforms that are consistent with their beliefs and ensuring the safety of their data regardless of whatever platform they decide to use.

Promoting media literacy and working to reduce the spread of false information

Responsibility and Procedures for Checking Facts

Independent fact-checking organizations should be required to work with social media platforms as part of regulations. The only way for platforms to detect and remove false or misleading information is to invest in AI-powered algorithms. To further encourage proactive measures and speedy reactions to incorrect information, harsh fines should be enforced on platforms who fail to address misinformation swiftly.

School Programs to Promote Media Literacy

Educating people is crucial to combating false information. School-based media literacy programs help students develop the critical thinking skills they'll need to evaluate material they find online, spot propaganda, and use the internet safely. Adults should also be the focus of education campaigns, since this will ensure that people in the future can identify trustworthy sources of information from those that are less so.

Internet Security and Protection against Cyberbullying

Comprehensive Legislation Against Cyberbullying

Comprehensive cyberbullying law that sets clear boundaries and legal repercussions for online abuse has to be a part of future policy. There needs to be a legal need for social media sites to include robust anti-cyberbullying measures, such as reporting tools, content monitoring, and prompt actions against bullies. Education initiatives should increase awareness about the emotional consequences of cyberbullying and promote empathy and respect online.

Victims of cyberbullying deserve government funding for specialized mental health services. Those who have been subjected to online harassment may find support through online platforms and mental health organizations that offer resources, therapy, and helplines. To help students build resilience against cyberbullying, schools should incorporate mental health education into their curricula.

Advancing Responsible Technology Use and Digital Citizenship
Learning About Digital Citizenship
To promote moral judgment, compassion, and tolerance in the digital space, schools should incorporate digital citizenship education into their curricula. The ramifications of their digital acts, as well as proper online conduct, should be taught to students. Future generations can benefit from positive online conversation and more welcoming online communities if digital citizenship is encouraged.

Ethical Principles in Social Media Platform Development
Legislation should push for the establishment of principles for the moral layout of online communities. These guidelines should discourage addictive features and content algorithms that amplify divisive or harmful information in favor of prioritizing the well-being of their users over engagement numbers. Platforms should fund studies to learn how their interfaces affect users' mental health so they can improve those outcomes.

V. Making Platforms Open and Responsible
Audits and Transparency Reports
Sites like Facebook, Twitter, and Instagram should be held accountable by mandating they release annual reports describing their content moderation, privacy policies, and anti-hate speech initiatives. If platforms are audited regularly by other parties, we know they're following the rules. Users and authorities can evaluate

how well platforms protect user privacy and security if they are provided with accurate data.

Government, Business, and Civil Society Working Together

Governments, social media companies, and non-governmental organizations (NGOs) must work together. To create policies that are both innovative and protect users, policymakers should consult with professionals in the field, academics, and members of civil society. Innovation in digital governance can be encouraged through public-private collaborations, making it more likely that rules will be flexible enough to keep up with the ever-changing digital context.

Conclusion

The widespread and varied effects of social media on modern society call for creative and flexible policy responses. Future rules can pave the road for a safer, more respectful digital environment by concentrating on privacy protection, fighting misinformation, preventing cyberbullying, encouraging digital citizenship, and assuring platform openness.

Working together, governments, corporations, and communities can create policies that put people in control, make platforms more accountable, and encourage responsible online behavior. The digital frontier can become a space where diversity, creativity, and respect thrive, shaping a more inclusive and empathetic world for generations to come if societies invest in education, technology, and ethical design to make the most of social media's enormous potential while mitigating its risks.

Chapter 6: The Future of Social Media and Cultural Influence

- **Speculation on the future trends in social media**
  The social media landscape is constantly shifting as a result of technological advancements and shifting user preferences. Looking ahead, it's certain that social media will further revolutionize our online modes of communication and sharing. This essay examines current developments and makes predictions about the future of social media by thinking about what might be next in terms of technology, user experience, and societal effects.

  First, I'll go over immersive technologies like VR and AR.
  Social Environments in Virtual Reality (VR)
  The potential for virtual reality to transform social media interactions cannot be overstated. Users of virtual reality social spaces will be able to communicate and collaborate in lifelike, three-dimensional settings. Users can participate in digital events, travel to new locations, and interact with their social networks without ever leaving their homes.

  What Augmented Reality (AR) Can Do for Online Shopping
  The future of internet shopping and consumer interaction with items is augmented reality. With augmented reality (AR) technologies built into social networking apps, customers may see items in context before making a purchase. Users will be able to create highly customized and engaging shopping experiences, from virtually putting on items to arranging furnishings in their living spaces.

  Voice-First and Audio-First Platforms
  Sound's Ascent

There has been a rise in popularity for "audio-first" systems, where users conduct most of their interactions through voice messages or real-time audio chats. These mediums allow for instantaneous, unplanned communication between users, fostering a more genuine bond between them. The success of Clubhouse, an audio-based social networking program, suggests a trend toward more interactive and conversation-focused networks.

Integration of Voice-Based Assistants into Social Life
In the near future, voice technology will be fully incorporated into social networking sites, thanks to AI-driven assistants like Amazon's Alexa and Apple's Siri. Voice commands can be used for a variety of social media interactions, including status updates and message delivery. The accessibility and usability of social networking platforms will be further improved by voice-driven content production capabilities that allow users to dictate posts, captions, and even podcasts.

Decentralized social networks and the blockchain
Free and Independent Social Networks
Blockchain-based decentralized social networks provide the possibility of greater user anonymity and data ownership. Users can choose what information to share and with whom, giving them a sense of agency over their data. Because of their resistance to censorship and their emphasis on transparency, decentralized networks inspire confidence in their users. The balance of power among users, platforms, and marketers may shift due to the proliferation of such networks.

Money Transfers and Cryptocurrencies
Transactions like tipping content producers, purchasing digital items, and donating to charity organizations might all be made easier with the help of cryptocurrency integration within social

media platforms. Tokens based on the blockchain have the potential to incentivise user activity and content production while also enabling individuals to directly monetise their social media profiles. These little purchases might significantly alter the creator economy by giving users new options to earn money from their online activities.

Artificial intelligence (AI) and tailor-made encounters
Hyper-Personalization
The algorithms underlying artificial intelligence will continue to develop, providing increasingly individualized services. In order to provide users with more relevant information streams, adverts, and suggestions, social media companies will monitor user behavior, preferences, and interactions. By tailoring recommendations to each individual user, AI-powered customization increases interaction and retention.

The Detection of Deep Fakes and the Validation of Content
Because of the increasing sophistication of deepfake technology, social media sites are investing in cutting-edge AI-driven solutions to identify and counteract falsified material. Users will be protected from misleading narratives and deceptive content thanks to AI systems that can detect deepfakes. There will also be content verification methods put in place to check user-generated content for accuracy and protect the reliability of social media.

Social media ethics and online health and safety
Wellness Functions for the User
By incorporating tools for digital detox, mindful usage, and mental health support, social media companies will put their users' health and happiness first. Users may better strike a balance between their online and offline lives with the help of tools like screen time management, activity tracking, and notifications for excessive

usage. A more responsible digital ecosystem will emerge as a result of social media platforms taking the initiative to address users' safety and mental health issues.

Transparency in Algorithms and Morality in AI

In the future, social media will devote more attention to the moral application of AI. Businesses will put money into open AI systems, helping customers see how algorithms select information to display. Fairness, accountability, and transparency will be at the forefront of ethical AI rules as they work to reduce bias and increase inclusion. If users can see how algorithms work, it will increase transparency and trust between platforms and their user base.

Conclusion

The future of social media promises a landscape replete with innovation, connectivity, and ethical considerations. From immersive technology altering our online interactions to decentralized networks redefining data ownership, social media's progress reflects our society's ever-changing digital requirements and goals.

There is plenty to look forward to with these emerging trends, but there are also ethical, privacy, and security concerns to consider. Both social media companies and government agencies will need to find a middle ground between user freedom and security. Accepting these developments responsibly will pave the way for a more inclusive, safe, and richer digital future as technology continues to weave its intricate tapestry into the fabric of our social relationships. The social media environment of the future will be shaped by society's ability to adapt to, innovate upon, and regulate these ever-developing technologies.

- **The role of emerging technologies (e.g., virtual reality, augmented reality) in shaping social media**

Emerging technologies are radically altering the way people communicate, share, and consume digital material, and this is having a significant impact on the social media environment. Immersive and interactive experiences that test conventional ideas of social interaction are at the forefront of the technological revolution ushered in by virtual reality (VR) and augmented reality (AR). In this article, we look at how VR and AR, two relatively new technologies, will play a major role in defining the future of social media. Understanding the changing face of online communication and connectivity requires diving into the possible uses, societal implications, and challenges of these technologies.

I. How VR Is Changing The Face Of Immersive Group Activities
VR Networking Sites
Social VR platforms have emerged in the wake of the VR revolution, providing a virtual setting for people to meet and talk to one another in real time. Socializing, gaming, and attending events in a virtual setting are all made possible by websites like VRChat and Facebook Horizon. With social VR, users may interact with their friends, family, and communities in ways that are strikingly similar to those they would have in real life. Social VR platforms are revolutionizing how we think about getting together with others online, whether for a party or to get work done.

Experiences and Live-Events in Virtual Reality
Virtual reality (VR) has the potential to revolutionize everything from concerts to conventions. Users can enjoy events like concerts and sporting events without leaving their homes if they have a virtual reality headset. Because of this democratization of access,

people from all over the world can take part in events as they happen. Virtual reality (VR) events are becoming increasingly popular since they allow viewers to feel as though they are in the same room as the artists.

Empathy in Virtual Reality

Because it allows users to feel what it's like to be in another person's shoes, virtual reality can be a powerful tool for teaching empathy. Virtual reality applications are being created to educate the public on pressing societal problems like poverty, inequality, and environmental degradation. Virtual reality (VR) promotes social change and activism by putting users in the shoes of others, fostering empathy and understanding. Social VR experiences have the potential to bridge gaps between cultures, encouraging empathy and compassion on a global scale.

Augmented reality (AR) to improve interactions in the real world
Social Augmented Reality Apps

Through the use of digital information and interactive components, augmented reality improves upon existing environments. Filters on social media apps like Snapchat and Instagram use augmented reality to add fun animations, effects, and virtual props to users' photographs and videos. These programs inspire users to let their imaginations run wild by letting them tailor their own material and broadcast exciting new adventures to their social circles.

With Augmented Reality in Online Shopping

By enabling consumers to envision things in their actual environments before making a purchase, augmented reality is revolutionizing the social commerce scene. The online shopping experience can be improved with the help of augmented reality try-on services for apparel, accessories, and cosmetics. Social commerce powered by augmented reality increases consumer trust, decreases product returns, and creates a more engaging and customized buying experience by bridging the gap between online and physical retail.

Augmented Reality for Exploration and Connection

The way people travel and discover new locations is revolutionized by navigation apps that use augmented reality. By providing immediate details on nearby attractions, eateries, and events, AR overlays enhance social interactions by making it easier for people to meet together unexpectedly. Users are more likely to explore their local areas and make new friends through the usage of augmented reality navigation apps.

Better Communication and Participation in Society

Virtual and augmented reality technologies have the potential to improve communication and broaden participation in society. Those who are physically unable to or who suffer from severe social anxiety may find that virtual reality makes it possible for them to take part in a wider range of social activities. Augmented reality apps that translate languages and showcase different cultures in real time let people of all walks of life communicate and learn from one another.

Issues of Confidentiality and Ethical Concerns

Data collecting, user tracking, and digital spying are all areas of worry when it comes to the immersive aspect of VR and AR. Ethical concerns about user consent and data security arise because virtual reality platforms need access to personal information like facial expressions and biometric data. Responsible deployment of these technologies in social media relies on finding a happy medium between individualized user experiences and user privacy.

Access Gaps and the Digital Divide

Widespread use of virtual reality and augmented reality is slowed by inequalities in cost and availability. Limited access to high-quality VR headsets and AR-enabled devices creates a digital gap, limiting underprivileged people from immersive social experiences. To ensure that a wide range of people can access and benefit from new technologies, we need programs that teach people how to use them, keep their costs down, and welcome everyone.

Conclusion

There will be a dramatic change in the way people communicate and engage online as a result of the widespread use of virtual and augmented reality features within social media platforms. These developing technologies provide unmatched opportunity to build immersive, engaging, and compassionate social experiences, exceeding the boundaries of standard digital communication. The ways in which we interact with one another are changing as a result of technological advancements like virtual reality and augmented reality.

The ethical, social, and accessibility issues raised by these technologies must be addressed as they develop further. The future of virtual and augmented reality technology relies on responsible innovation, user privacy regulations, and attempts to bridge access inequities in order to advance digital equity and improve people's social connections. By capitalizing on the disruptive power of new technologies, social media may develop into a vibrant and welcoming community where people from all walks of life can have their voices heard, relationships can grow deeper, and empathy can be nurtured, ultimately leading to a more connected and empathetic online society.

- **Ethical considerations and potential positive and negative outcomes**

  New ethical questions arise with the introduction of cutting-edge technology like virtual reality (VR) and augmented reality (AR) to social media sites. As society adopts these revolutionary technologies, it is crucial to analyze the moral implications and plan for both the good and the bad outcomes. This essay delves into the potential benefits and drawbacks of using virtual reality and augmented reality in social media from an ethical standpoint.

  New Technologies and Ethical Considerations I.
  Confidentiality of User Information
  The protection of individual privacy is a major issue for VR and AR developers. Sensitive information, such as biometric data and user behavior patterns, is frequently gathered by these devices. Strong data security measures, open data practices, and user consent are essential for protecting user privacy. Protecting users' privacy from intrusion is a top priority for ethical virtual reality and augmented reality platforms.

  The Effects of Technology on Mental Health
  The immersive quality of VR and AR experiences raises concerns about digital addiction and its influence on mental health. Addiction-like behaviors may develop from extended usage of virtual worlds, which can have negative consequences for users' relationships and health in the real world. Designing technologies that promote responsible usage, digital detox, and user-monitoring features is important from an ethical perspective because it helps people maintain a healthy, well-rounded relationship with technology.

  Moderating Content and Falsehoods

VR and AR systems encounter problems relating to content control and misinformation. Since these tools make it easier than ever for people to produce and distribute immersive content, verifying the veracity of claims is more important than ever. Misinformation, hate speech, and harmful content may and should be addressed with the use of ethical content moderation systems. Careful ethical deliberation and open rules are necessary for finding a middle ground between free speech and limiting the spread of damaging information.

Part Two: The Upside: Cultivating Compassion and Tolerance
Connecting Emotion and Digital Reality
Virtual reality has the ability to increase people's capacity for empathy by exposing them to novel situations. Users can gain empathy and understanding of the struggles of underrepresented groups using virtual reality applications that imitate the experiences of those groups. Virtual reality (VR) helps people connect with one another across social and cultural boundaries by putting them in the shoes of another person.

Interactions That Include Everyone
By increasing access and inclusion, augmented reality technologies improve social interactions. With the help of augmented reality software, people who speak different languages can communicate more effectively. Accessibility elements can also be included as an augmented reality overlay to help those with mobility impairments get around. These accessible technologies foster greater social harmony by making the world more welcoming to people of all abilities.

Negative Consequences: Threats and Obstacles
Disconnect from reality and the lure of digital devices

The danger of digital escapism arises as a result of the attractiveness of immersive technologies, as users avoid real-world interactions and obligations in favor of the safety and comfort of virtual ones. Users' mental health, social lives, and relationships may all suffer as a result of this detachment from reality. Ethical concerns should center on striking a good balance between fully immersing oneself in a virtual environment and keeping a meaningful connection to the actual world.

Privacy Violating Augmented Reality

Privacy issues have been voiced in relation to augmented reality applications, especially those that make use of facial recognition technology. Users run the possibility of having their personal information collected without their knowledge, which poses privacy and surveillance problems. Transparent data usage standards, strong permission systems, and legislation that secure persons from improper data collection are required to strike a balance between creative AR applications and user privacy.

Harmonizing New Technologies' Innovative Potential with Its Ethical Obligations

Responsible innovation and user-centered design are especially crucial in light of the ethical questions raised by technologies like virtual reality and augmented reality. Stakeholders including technology developers, politicians, and users must work together to construct ethical frameworks that promote user well-being, privacy, and diversity as society navigates the complexity of incorporating new technologies into social media.

By developing ethical practices, promoting openness, and stressing user education, society may harness the beneficial potential of VR and AR while reducing the bad repercussions. To shape a digital future that is both inventive and morally responsible, we need to find a middle ground between the two. This will ensure that these revolutionary technologies positively contribute to social connections, empathy, and inclusivity.

- **Reflection on the book's main themes and a call to action for readers to engage critically with social media and its cultural implications**

   Individuals and communities alike need to be equipped with the knowledge and skills necessary to critically engage with the complexities of the ever-changing social media ecosystem. In this analysis, we'll delve into the book's key topics, discussing the transformative potential and occasional drawbacks of social media. It sends a call to action to readers to navigate the digital world with responsibility and thoughtfulness, stressing the significance of active, critical interaction with these platforms.

I. Exploring Themes in the Digital Environment
The Cultural Impact of Social Media
As a result of its pervasiveness and influence, social media sites have become a focal point for contemporary culture. Social media is a barometer of the times, picking up on everything from viral trends to online movements, giving a voice to the voiceless and shaping cultural standards. Understanding social media's position as a cultural phenomena is vital for comprehending its impact on individual identities and society ideals.

Crossroads of Culture and Technology
Complex dynamics emerge at the crossroads of technology and culture, influencing our worldviews, social interactions, and sense of self. By bringing people together from all walks of life, social media sites create a digital tapestry that represents the richness of the human experience. Investigating this connection sheds light on the complex nature of social media's reach.

Moral and Ethical Issues

Privacy, false information, cyberbullying, and the digital divide are only some of the ethical and moral concerns related to social media. Responsible content production, consumption, and platform utilization are all essential in overcoming these moral obstacles. Social media users are more likely to participate thoughtfully, with consideration for the rights and well-being of others, if the ethical components of these platforms are recognized.

Part II: The Responsibility of the Reader for Introspection and Evaluation

Building Computer Skills and Knowledge

For critical participation in social media, digital literacy is essential. It equips people to recognize biases online, evaluate the veracity of content, and use digital tools safely. Readers are urged to make an effort to improve their digital literacy so that they can use social media with critical thinking and discernment.

Putting Prejudices and Assumptions to the Test

Reflecting on one's assumptions and prejudices is crucial when dealing with social media. Many online communities serve as echo chambers that reinforce users' preexisting worldviews by reflecting and reinforcing their own views. Readers are encouraged to question their assumptions, seek out alternative points of view, and interact with material that makes them question their worldview. Individuals can increase their knowledge of the world and their capacity for empathy through the process of questioning assumptions.

Examining the origins, biases, and goals of the stuff you come across online is an important part of consuming social media content mindfully. The significance of one's personal online profile is further highlighted by the practice of mindful participation. The content a reader shares should be carefully considered for its potential consequences and checked against ethical principles. Contributions with depth enrich online conversation, leading to greater understanding and friendship.

Fostering Compassion and Dignity in the Digital Age

The cornerstone of responsible online behavior is digital empathy, the capacity to comprehend and share the emotions of others online. The authors encourage the audience to practice empathy in their online interactions by seeing the person behind every profile image and user name. By practicing digital empathy, users can help create a more positive virtual community and reduce the prevalence of toxic speech on social media.

Promoting Moral Conduct in Online Communities

Advocating for moral conduct on social media means pressing companies to explain their algorithms, policies, and content moderation processes. Readers are urged to speak up for openness, individual privacy, and ethical AI development. Positive change in the social media landscape can be pushed forward by participating in discussions, lending support to ethical efforts, and increasing knowledge of digital ethics.

Promoting Online Counseling and Training

The development of ethical online behavior relies heavily on guidance and instruction from trusted adults. Readers are urged to play a role as role models for younger generations by teaching them to think critically, become media literate, and act ethically when using the internet. Individuals can be better equipped to use social media responsibly if they are exposed to educational initiatives that encourage digital literacy. Mentoring and education can help raise a new generation of online citizens that are well-informed, compassionate, and conscientious.

Conclusion

Individuals in the modern information era have a duty, not a choice, to critically engage with social media and its cultural ramifications. This analysis shows that the book's topics highlight the significance of considerate communication, ethical considerations, and the development of digital empathy. The digital landscape can be actively shaped by readers by encouraging them to reflect on their own digital habits, question assumptions, and advocate for ethical social media.

By responding to the reflection's call to action, readers will play a crucial role in building a digital culture that is more welcoming, compassionate, and ethically sound. Individuals can transform online relationships by using critical awareness and ethical principles to navigate the intricacies of social media, so establishing a digital world characterized by compassion, respect, and responsible digital citizenship.

Conclusion

- ## Summarization of the key points from each chapter

    Examining the far-reaching effects of digital communication on cultures worldwide, "Social Media and Cultural Influence: Trends and Implications" dives into the complex relationship between social media and cultural dynamics. This synopsis captures the essence of the work, providing an accessible introduction to the themes and ideas it develops.

    First Chapter: How Social Media Influences Popular Culture
    The first chapter introduces the essential relationship between social media and culture. Digital platforms are emphasized as cultural hubs that both reflect and shape prevailing social mores, customs, and expressions. This chapter focuses on how the democratization of cultural narratives has made it possible for a wider range of perspectives to be shared, appreciated, and archived. Central to this issue is the concept of cultural globalization, where social media fosters the sharing of ideas, customs, and values on a worldwide scale.

    Language Change in the Internet Era
    The revolutionary effects of social media on the development of languages are explored in Chapter 2. Shortcuts for online communication are discussed, with an emphasis on how emoticons and acronyms have become standard features of online discourse. The concept of "internet language" and the role that social media platforms have had in the development of new idioms and phrases are discussed in this chapter. This highlights the unique linguistic characteristics of different communities and the cultural diversity inherent in digital languages.

Culture and the Internet as a Medium for Self-Expression

In this chapter, we explore the complicated web that forms between cultural identity and the use of digital media to convey ideas. It looks at how people are using online communities to express, investigate, and celebrate their cultural identities. The chapter explains how online networks can help preserve indigenous knowledge, unite people of different backgrounds, and instill a sense of pride in one's heritage. It highlights how social media gives underrepresented groups a voice, empowering them to confront bias and disseminate alternative viewpoints.

Culture shifts and social media celebrities make up Chapter 4.
The rise of social media stars as cultural leaders is the subject of Chapter 4. It studies how influencers drive consumer behavior, influence fashion choices, and effect cultural preferences. This chapter delves into the moral quandaries inherent in influencer marketing, placing special emphasis on the role that influencers must play in fostering an atmosphere of genuine cultural appreciation. The role of influential people in promoting social justice, cultural continuity, and acceptance is also emphasized.

Digital cultural expression presents unique difficulties and obligations (Chapter 5).
In the third section, we explore the risks and rewards of cultural expression in the digital sphere. Topics covered include cultural theft, digital colonialism, and the commercialization of historical artifacts. This chapter stresses the importance of appropriate cultural representation by digital platforms, content makers, and users. Among the topics covered are cultural awareness, IP rights, and the moral use of cultural symbols in online environments.

Social media and cultural complexity: a last reflection

In sum, "Social Media and Cultural Influence: Trends and Implications" offers a deep dive into the complex web of connections between social media and different cultural traditions. It exemplifies the way in which internet platforms are reshaping language tendencies, cultural identities, and international interactions. The book stresses the significance of cultural appreciation and ethical participation in the digital era, as well as the importance of being a good digital citizen.

In order to promote cultural awareness, empathy, and acceptance in one's online interactions, the book's authors advise readers to carefully consider the complex ideas provided. Individuals may help create a digital world where different cultural expressions are appreciated, respected, and conserved for years to come by navigating the complicated landscape of social media and culture with awareness and sensitivity.

- **Final thoughts on the evolving relationship between social media and culture**

    The ways in which cultures interact, express themselves, and define themselves have been revolutionized by the rapid development of the connection between social media and popular culture. There are profound ramifications to consider as we stand at the crossroads of technological progress and cultural variety. This essay delves into some concluding ideas on the complex relationship between social media and culture, with a focus on the prospects, perils, and obligations that lie ahead in this revolutionary process.

    I. Freedom of Expression and Cultural Agency
    We can now express ourselves freely across cultures using social media. They give underrepresented groups a global platform to tell their stories and spread their ideas. The global reach of social media facilitates the preservation of indigenous traditions and the reconnection of diaspora populations with their homelands. This increasing confidence encourages people to publicly embrace their background and celebrate their cultural traditions. By removing physical borders and fostering communication across cultures, the internet has become a fertile ground for artistic expression.

    The Digital Age and Cultural Heritage Preservation
    The preservation of cultural heritage in the digital age faces both new opportunities and new obstacles. Online communities document cultural practices and linguistic varieties that might otherwise be lost to the sands of time. Online groups dedicated to cultural preservation actively curate content, assuring the transmission of knowledge to future generations. But there are also questions concerning the veracity of cultural portrayal in the digital realm. The commodification, misrepresentation, and appropriation of culture all pose risks to its survival. Striking a balance between

sharing cultural knowledge and honoring its sanctity is vital to preserve cultural heritage ethically and responsibly.

Third, International Relations through the Medium of Culture
By facilitating communication and collaboration on a global scale, social media has revolutionized cultural diplomacy. Digital platforms have opened up new venues for cultural exchange programs, artistic collaborations, and virtual exhibitions, all of which contribute to greater cross-cultural understanding. Dispelling preconceived notions, online encounters introduce people to new points of view. Cultural diplomacy fueled by social media promotes understanding, compassion, and gratitude for the variety of human expression around the world.

IV. Obstacles and Moral Concerns
Despite exciting prospects, the dynamic between social media and culture also presents formidable obstacles. The digital realm is rife with problems such as cultural appropriation, stereotyping, and the warping of traditions. The commercial exploitation of cultural symbols creates moral questions and calls for more conscientious content production and consumption. In addition, false information and damaging prejudices can spread rapidly through social media. Digital literacy, cultural sensitivity, and ethical principles that account for the nuance of cultural expression are necessary to overcome these obstacles.

Change and Social Protest in the Age of Technology
Individuals and groups have been given a voice to fight for cultural and social justice through the use of social media, which has emerged as a catalyst for digital activism and social change. The digital space has become a rallying point for cultural preservation, indigenous rights, and diversity and inclusion initiatives. The voices of activists calling for societal change and criticizing repressive

conventions are amplified through the use of hashtags, viral campaigns, and internet petitions. The internet is a democratic platform for cultural activists to build coalitions, spread information, and effect global change.

The Implications of Digital Technology on Social and Cultural Interactions

The future is bright because of the transformative potential of the developing connection between social media and culture. Technologies like augmented reality (AR) and virtual reality (VR) have the potential to radically alter the way people engage with art, history, and tradition. AI-driven language translation systems will promote seamless communication among varied linguistic communities, increasing cross-cultural understanding. Potential concerns with cultural ownership and intellectual property rights could be resolved through the use of blockchain technology, leading to more equitable recompense for cultural creators.

Furthermore, encouraging tolerance and diversity is crucial for the future of social media. All voices should be heard and platforms should make it a top priority, especially those from underrepresented groups. Content moderation policies should be considerate of different cultures so that they can successfully combat issues like bigotry and stereotyping. Initiatives to foster cultural diversity, protect cultural heritage, and combat stereotyping can be propelled by cooperation between social media platforms, cultural groups, and activists.

Conclusion

The way people interact, share information, and live together in modern society has been fundamentally altered by the dynamic between social media and culture. Accepting this change calls for a unified dedication to cultural sensitivity, empathy, and moral action.

Cultural diversity, preservation of tradition, and the promotion of inclusive online spaces where every voice is heard and respected are of paramount importance as we negotiate the intricacies of the digital age.

We can pave the path for a future where cultural connections are valued, understood, and accepted by leveraging the revolutionary potential of social media while realizing its constraints. The complex web of possibilities presented by the interplay between social media and culture in the modern digital age encourages us to create a story of mutual understanding, appreciation, and compassion. As citizens of the world, we have the power to create a society where many cultures thrive and complement one another.

- **The lasting impact of social media on society and the importance of responsible use.**

   Without a doubt, the proliferation of social media has altered the very foundations of society, revolutionizing the ways in which people interact with one another and understand the world around them. It has permeated many facets of our life, both positively and negatively. This essay explores the long-term effects of social media on culture and stresses the critical role that responsible usage plays in today's information society. The importance of encouraging ethical and contemplative engagement in the digital era becomes clearer when we consider the far-reaching effects of social media on interpersonal connections, psychological well-being, political participation, and the spread of knowledge.

   Relationships and Social Media, Part I
   The advent of social media platforms has changed the nature of human interactions by breaking down barriers of distance and time. The potential for these platforms to facilitate meaningful connections is commensurate with the obstacles they provide. A digital social sphere has emerged as a result of the widespread use of social media, one in which personal boundaries are sometimes blurred, privacy is frequently breached, and in-person relationships are sometimes forgone in favor of virtual ones. Finding a happy medium between online and offline contacts, protecting your own and others' privacy, and considering how your online behaviors may affect your offline relationships are all part of responsible use.

   Mental Health and Online Communities
   There are several facets to the intricate relationship between social media use and psychological well-being. One positive aspect of online social networks is their role as meeting places for mutual aid and information sharing in the realm of mental health. However, it has been linked to problems including cyberbullying, social

comparison, and digital addiction, all of which can have serious consequences for mental health. Responsible use of social media requires self-awareness, digital detoxification when necessary, and encouraging online places that prioritize empathy, positivism, and mental health awareness. Users need to keep an eye on their screen time and be aware of any bad effects it may be having on their psyche.

Thirdly, the Impact of Social Media on Politics
There is no denying the impact that social media has had on politics and public opinion. Online communities like these have evolved into potent instruments for political activity, public education campaigns, and bottom-up movements. At the same time, problems like echo chambers, fake news, and polarization have been associated with social media. Critical thinking, fact checking, and media literacy are all essential for the ethical use of social media in politics. In order to achieve a well-rounded comprehension of intricate topics, users must take part in educated political discourse, be cognizant of their own prejudices, and actively seek out the viewpoints of others.

Dissemination of Knowledge through Social Media
Media like Facebook and Twitter have leveled the playing field when it comes to getting information out to the public. However, problems like the proliferation of fake news, conspiracy theories, and disinformation have emerged as a result of the speed and accessibility of information on social media. Media literacy, source evaluation, and a dedication to spreading only factually sound information are all necessary for responsible use in this setting. Users need to exercise critical thinking skills by challenging claims made and supporting reputable media outlets.

Using Technology Appropriately and Promoting Digital Literacy

Promoting ethical use of social media demands a comprehensive approach to digital literacy and education. Integrating digital literacy programs into K-12 curriculums equips the next generation with the critical thinking skills necessary to thrive in today's information-rich world. Further, people of all ages should constantly educate themselves on how to protect themselves online, how to control their personal information, and how to spot fake news. Mindful consumption, healthy boundaries, and awareness of potential consequences all play a part in responsible tech use.

When it comes to encouraging ethical behavior online, social media businesses play a key role. Ethical social media networks must have clear algorithms, strict content moderation procedures, and preventative efforts to counteract disinformation. In addition, it is imperative that these platforms put the safety, security, and privacy of its users first. When it comes to the social effect of their platforms, ethical tech businesses do more than just talk the talk; they walk the walk.

Conclusion

The lasting impact of social media on society is evident, altering how we connect, share, and interpret the world. The digital environment of the future is in part determined by our generation's responsible use of these platforms. We can take use of the benefits of social media while minimizing its drawbacks if we help people become more technologically literate, encourage them to think critically, and encourage them to engage in ethical behavior.

By acting as good digital citizens, we can shape a future online where mutual regard and cooperation are the norm. To make a positive and long-lasting impact on ourselves, our peers, and the world at large, we must acknowledge the importance of responsible social media use and participate actively in creating a digital society guided by ethical values.

- **Encouragement for readers to continue exploring this dynamic field**

It's exciting to see the ever-changing environment of social media evolve, with its extraordinary inventions and societal transformations. This essay is meant to serve as a motivator for readers to continue exploring the fascinating and ever-changing world of digital interactions. Readers can not only keep up with the newest developments but also contribute significantly to the shaping of this transformational realm by embracing curiosity, fostering digital literacy, and actively engaging with the many facets of social media.

I. How Curiosity Keeps Us Exploring the Universe
The urge to know more is what motivates explorers. In the arena of social media, curiosity pushes users to ask probing questions, discover new trends, and seek inventive answers. The gateway to new platforms, technology, and social media phenomena is opened by embracing this inquisitiveness. Readers are urged to explore multiple social media channels, from visual platforms like Instagram and TikTok to professional networks like LinkedIn, each giving distinct experiences and insights into different parts of human connection.

Increasing Opportunities for Informed Exploration in the Digital Age
In today's digital age, the ability to read and write digital content is crucial for any serious researcher. Digital literacy includes skills such as understanding how social media algorithms function, spotting fake news, and being familiar with online privacy settings. In order to effectively evaluate information, locate trustworthy resources, and traverse the digital landscape, readers are urged to make an investment in their digital education. Readers can improve their digital literacy through a number of available online courses,

workshops, and resources, giving them the tools they need to confidently and critically navigate the online world.

Taking in New Ideas and Worldviews (Third Aim)
The world's many peoples, customs, and philosophies find common ground in the realm of social media. Readers are offered a rich tapestry of human experiences and perspectives when they actively engage with this diversity. By keeping up with prominent figures in diverse fields, cultures, and economies, readers can learn about new markets, social movements, and international issues. Readers' experiences in the digital world are enriched when they are exposed to content from a variety of perspectives and perspectives.

In-Depth Investigation of the Social Effects of Social Media
Readers are urged to go beyond superficial connections and conduct in-depth research into the societal effects of social media. Learning more about the cultural, psychological, and political effects of social media requires reading scholarly articles, research papers, and books. Readers can learn more about issues including digital communication ethics, social media psychology, the importance of social media in political movements, and online activism. Reading scholarly discourse broadens the horizons of its audience, allowing them to more accurately assess social media phenomena and contribute intelligently to pertinent conversations.

Engaged Creation and Active Participation in Exploration
Social media is not only a platform for passive consumption; it is a space for active interaction and production. Readers are urged to join debates, provide their own insights, and start new threads in online communities. The ability to express oneself creatively and participate in the ongoing digital conversation is enhanced when readers create their own content in the form of blog entries, podcasts, videos, or other visual art. A sense of community is

fostered and an exploratory, collaborative attitude is encouraged when people take part in discussions, make insightful comments, and work together.

Exploration with Responsibility while Facing Ethical Difficulties

When delving into the world of social media, one must also deal with moral dilemmas. Readers are urged to treat their online relationships with honesty, compassion, and courtesy. Avoiding cyberbullying and respecting personal space are only two examples of why it's important to be self-aware when using the internet. Exploration with a sense of responsibility entails things like giving thought to the moral consequences of using social media, backing efforts to improve people's experiences online, and promoting moral behavior online. By discussing and working through difficult ethical questions, readers help foster a safe, welcoming space online.

Conclusion

The ever-evolving world of social media provides a limitless playground for curiosity, innovation, and education. Readers can go on an enriching voyage of discovery if they cultivate their curiosity, learn to use technology effectively, seek out and consider alternative points of view, conduct thorough research, and join and contribute to online communities. Exploration that is based on ethical values and mutual respect not only improves the quality of users' individual experiences, but also helps the digital community as a whole grow and develop.

Readers are urged to keep an open mind, a critical eye, and a kind heart as they delve more into this ever-evolving topic. A future where meaningful relationships, creativity, and empathy flourish will be shaped by readers who accept the complexity of social media and actively participate in its continual evolution. In this spirit of discovery, readers are encouraged to brave the online world with a sense of wonder, an open mind, and a determination to participate in it in a way that is both responsible and ethical.

www.ingramcontent.com/pod-product-compliance
Lightning Source LLC
LaVergne TN
LVHW020450070526
838199LV00063B/4899